The Envy of Eve truly is a wonderful book – with a deeply biblical perspective into the sinful human heart and with practical guidance towards a life of godliness and holiness. I found myself underlining the manuscript as I went along! In her book, Melissa Kruger uncovers the deepest machinations of the human heart, revealing how covetousness, lust, and greed are tempting doors of departure from the path of godliness. By focusing on Biblical truths and examples, Kruger opens our eyes to the scope and depth of covetousness in our lives, while also drawing us into the path of holiness and a life honoring and glorifying God. The questions at the end of each of the chapters make this a perfect tool for personal as well as group Bible study.

Diana Lynn Severance
Author of *Feminine Threads* and Historian, Spring, Texas

To read *The Envy of Eve* is to gaze into a mirror reflecting the covetousness latent in the human heart. With skill and insight Melissa Kruger exposes the fault lines that as Christian women we know are there but are all too often ashamed to admit. Yet we are not left to thrash around in helpless despair. Through biblical examples and sympathetic counsel we are pointed again and again to the delivering power of the Lord Jesus Christ.

Faith Cook
Author of *Troubled Journey,* Derbyshire, England

With I've-been-there understanding and been-in-the-Word insight, Melissa Kruger helps us to look beneath the surface of our discontent, exposing our covetous hearts to the healing light of God's Word. The Bible-saturated study ably applies the gospel to an area many of us have never invited it to go to work.

Nancy Guthrie
Author of the *Seeing Jesus in the Old Testament Bible Study* series, Nashville, Tennessee

We live in an age where governments are teetering because of a sinful, self-centred sense of entitlement by the populace. Furthermore, we live in an age when individuals, particularly in the West, are constantly comparing themselves with others, and there is a relentless pursuit of materialism, which, as we know, can never truly satisfy. In the midst of this veritable cauldron of lust and sinful desires, there is a need to go back to the simple understanding of what the Scriptures call 'covetousness'. I am thankful for this new book by my friend Melissa Kruger which not only helps us come to terms with this disease of the soul, but also, mercifully, offers a remedy. Mrs Kruger's insights are grounded in the Scriptures, the Reformed confessions, and her own wise diagnosis, reflections and helpful treatment of the diabolical maladies of our age. I commend this fine, new book by Melissa with a prayer that we all read and follow her Biblical counsel to fully understand the condition we are in and flee quickly to the One who truly satisfies our deepest longings and our true desires.

Michael A. Milton

President and Senior Fellow,

D. James Kennedy Institute for Christianity and Culture.

In an age and culture where we all tend to have an overdeveloped sense of entitlement, this book makes a brilliant diagnosis that goes right to the heart of the problem. It combines a well-structured, analytical approach worthy of the best of the Puritan writers with a fresh and well-illustrated understanding of the way contemporary women think. The applications of Biblical truth are completely fearless and absolutely spot-on.

Ann Benton

Wife to John Benton, Managing Editor of *Evangelicals Now.*

Guildford, England

The Envy of Eve gets to the root of our struggle for contentment. It's not our circumstances that need transformation – it's our hearts. With empathy and grounded biblical insight, Melissa Kruger shows us the path to abiding joy amidst life's varied 'ups' and 'downs'.

Lydia Brownback

Author of *Contentment,* Wheaton, Illinois

The Envy of Eve

Finding Contentment in a Covetous World

Melissa B. Kruger

paperback ISBN 978-1-84550-775-6
epub ISBN 978-1-84550-944-6
mobi ISBN 978-1-84550-945-3

10 9 8 7 6 5 4 3 2 1

First published in 2012,
reprinted in 2012, 2014, 2016, 2017 and 2018
by
Christian Focus Publications,
Geanies House, Fearn,
Ross-shire, IV20 1TW, Scotland
www.christianfocus.com

Cover design by Paul Lewis

Printed by Bell and Bain

CONTENTS

Acknowledgements

In his first letter to the Corinthians, Paul asks, 'What do you have that you did not receive?'[1] In the writing of this book, I have been blessed to receive. It seems at every turn, God faithfully brought the right person, the right passage of Scripture or the perfect quote to spur me on in thinking, writing and endurance. Seeing His guiding hand and tender mercies were the greatest personal blessing for me as I wrote.

My parents have supported me throughout the years by investing so much of their lives into my life. I can never thank them enough for all of their encouragement, hard work and love. My brother Rob challenges me by his example and his encouragement. He also gave me a wonderful friend and sister-in-law, Dottie, to discuss these topics with over the sound of many children's voices. Mike's family supports us in so many ways. We could not do these writing projects without weekend trips allowing the kids to visit Opa and Grandma.

1 1 Corinthians 4:7

Two friends, Catriona Anderson and Angela Queen, read every page and gave me great insight along the way. I am thankful for the gift of their time and editing wisdom. Heather Jones and Scott Suddreth also read parts of this manuscript and gave helpful suggestions. I am thankful for their gift of making me laugh in the sometimes tedious editing process.

Much of this book was written while we were living in Cambridge, England. I am appreciative to Tyndale House for allowing me access to their library and providing a quiet place to write and reflect. I am also grateful to Jessica Dean for living with our family in Hawthorne House and loving on our children while I was writing.

Kate MacKenzie at Christian Focus has been an encouraging supporter of this project from the beginning. Rebecca Rine faithfully edited the text and offered excellent improvements. I am thankful to both of them for their efforts in publishing this book.

I am blessed to have friends who faithfully prayed for this project. Thank you to Macon Collins, Peggy Chapman, Anne Rogers, Beth Herring, Kate Stewart, Tracy Thornton, Erica Crumpler, Teresa Davis, Kimberly Curlin, and Lisa Marie Ferguson for praying for me and sharing life with me. Thank you to Shanna Davis for her faithful encouragement from Prague. I think Connice Dyar may have listened to me speak on this topic more than anyone else and each time she still found something encouraging to say. Her words spurred me on to keep writing. Thank you to the ladies at Wednesday Morning Bible Study and the staff of Uptown Church for your prayers and support of this book. A few women also took the time (and had the courage) to share their own stories of coveting. Thank you for being willing to open up and let others have a first-hand view into the painful consequences of coveting.

Most importantly, God supplied my family to faithfully encourage and support me. My children, Emma, John and

Kate gave me needed breaks from the writing process. They fill my life with such rich blessings and allow me the opportunity to observe and reflect upon the immeasurable love of God. My husband Mike provided insight, clarity, encouragement, and time to write. He faithfully read every page and challenged me to go deeper in my thinking, while cheering me on in the process. I have received so much and am thankful for the many prayers and words of encouragement!

To Mike

I am so thankful to share this journey with you.

'Where you go I will go, and where you stay I will stay'
(Ruth 1:16)

Happiness does not lie in abundance, but in the suitableness of our mind to our estate (Luke 12:15). There is a twofold war in man: the war between a man and his conscience which breeds trouble of the mind, and a war between his affections and his condition which breeds murmuring and envious grumbling. So, pray for contentment also when you pray 'Give us this day our daily bread.'

THOMAS MANTON

Voices From the Past, ed. Richard Rushing
(Edinburgh: Banner of Truth Trust, 2009), p. 124.

Introduction

When I look back over the past year, I'm not quite sure how this book got written. The fact that it is in your hands now amazes me more than anyone. In the midst of writing, I was busy being a mom to three children, ages two to eight. I began a new part-time job at our church helping with women's ministry. We packed up our home and moved internationally for four and a half months to Cambridge, England for my husband's sabbatical. The circumstances of my life were not favorable to beginning a new endeavor. However, it became clear through different opportunities that the Lord wanted me to write about the lessons He had been teaching me over the past fifteen years of life and ministry with my husband.

Most of what you'll find in this book comes from years of daily prayer and Bible study that began in my early teens. Throughout the years, the most important moments of my life have been spent with my Bible open and my journal before me for prayer. In those moments, the Lord has given life to my living and joy to my heart. At each stage along the way, He has also given me opportunities to study the

Bible with other women. A few years ago, I led a study on the book of Joshua. It was during this study that I first dealt with the story of Achan and the effects of his covetous behavior. The next fall, I had the opportunity to speak at our church's Women's Retreat, dealing with the topic of coveting and how it eats away at our joy and contentment. These opportunities laid the foundation that led to further study and consideration of how to find joy in the midst of life's unexpected twists and turns.

What I was studying in the Bible during those years was also colliding with the circumstances of my life. Slowly, I became aware of the fact that I was, in many ways, living the traditional 'American Dream'. I met and married my college boyfriend. After many years of school, he was teaching as a Professor of New Testament at Reformed Theological Seminary. It was a job and a city that we had both dreamed about for years. At this point, we had two healthy children – a girl and a boy (the third came along a couple of years later). We bought our first home and developed many close friendships. If one simply looked at the outside of my life, all looked well.

In reality, I faced struggles and hardships just like anyone else. Hurts and pain came into my life through relational struggles, sin struggles, physical ailments and unmet expectations. Also, at each stage of 'gaining' – a husband, children, job, home, and friends – I experienced the reality that acquiring more did not necessarily satisfy or give me contentment. Often, living the life for which I had hoped proved to be more difficult in reality than I imagined it in my dreams.

As I met and got to know other women, I realized that I was not alone in this experience. Our church is full of relatively wealthy, educated and attractive women who appear to have everything the world has to offer. Yet, as

I have met with woman after woman, and the masks have come off, I often find a very different reality underneath the outward picture of perfection. Inside each heart resides deep longings. Some long for more possessions, others long for healthy relationships, while still others long for a different season of life. Most are longing for good things, wondering deep within their hearts, 'Has God forgotten about me?'. As they look over the fence into others' seemingly content lives, it can appear that the grass is greener and slowly, unbelief about God's goodness creeps into the heart.

Once this seed of unbelief takes root, the weed of covetousness sprouts. As it grows, the fruit of the spirit – love, joy, peace, patience, kindness, goodness, faithfulness, gentleness and self-control[1] – is often choked out. Covetousness leaves little room for anything healthy to grow and blooms into a life of discontentment. While much has been written about the various idols we worship, very little has been written about the covetous desires that lead us into idolatry. God's good gifts can become idols when the depth of our desire for them becomes inordinate. The hope of this book is to expose the sin of covetousness, showing the truth of Proverbs 14:30, 'A heart at peace gives life to the body, but envy rots the bones.'

The first section of the book, chapters 1–4, deals with understanding the sin of coveting. We will look at what coveting is (and what it is not), explore the reasons we covet, observe the pattern it takes in the stories of Eve and Achan, and finally, look to Christ for a new pattern to put on by His power at work in our hearts to fight our covetous tendencies. In the second section of the book, chapters 5–9, we will consider five particular areas in which we often tend to struggle with covetous desires. We will examine our longings for

---

1 Galatians 5:22

money and possessions, romantic relationships, friendships and familial relationships, seasons and circumstances, and giftedness and abilities. In each of these areas, we will study a Biblical character who struggled with that particular covetous desire. Hopefully, as we study their negative examples, we will learn the wisdom of Paul's warning to the church at Corinth: 'Now these things occurred as examples to keep us from setting our hearts on evil things as they did... These things happened to them as examples and were written down as warnings for us, on whom the fulfillment of the ages has come. So, if you think you are standing firm, be careful that you don't fall!'[2]

At the end of each chapter are questions that can be used for individual or group study and reflection. Many times, digging deep into our desires exposes the various ways we attempt to live life apart from abiding in Christ. As you observe and reflect upon these topics, I encourage you to seek out others with whom to pray through and discuss these issues. The goal is to expose the harmful results of this sin pattern in our lives. As we turn the light on and see the effects of this sin on our hearts, once again we realize our overwhelming need for Christ. We will not be able to let go of our affections for the world's goods until we grow in our affection for Christ. Psalm 119 offers an excellent prayer for each of us as we begin:

> Incline my heart to your testimonies,
> and not to selfish gain!
> Turn my eyes from looking at worthless things;
> and give me life in your ways.[3]

---

2 1 Corinthians 10:6 -12

3 Psalm 119: 36-37, ESV

1 *The Cry of the Covetous*

O! beware, my lord, of jealousy;
It is the green-eyed monster which doth mock
The meat it feeds on;

WILLIAM SHAKESPEARE

Othello, Act 3, Scene 3.

1

The Cry of the Covetous:

'Life's Not Fair!'

'*It's not fair!*' I often wonder how many times those words rolled off my tongue during childhood. I grew up with one brother, Rob, and as children often do, we spent much of our childhood comparing our situations. If one of us got a new toy, the other would also expect a new toy. If one of us got to go to a neighbor's house to play, the other wanted a friend to come over and play at our house. If he was allowed to jump on the neighbor's new trampoline, then it seemed fair that I should also be allowed to jump. He was three years older than me, so by virtue of his age, he naturally had more freedom. However, I was sometimes allowed to do things at an earlier age, because he was with me (and, as usually happens, I'm sure my parents relaxed more with the second child). He might claim it was unfair that I was allowed to watch a certain movie at age eleven, because he saw it for the first time when he was twelve. I might claim it was unfair that he got to spend the night at a friend's house, forgetting that he was three years older and most likely my parents would afford me the same privilege when I was older. I even remember comparing the chores we were required to do around the house. I was convinced vacuuming (of course, it was Rob's chore) was much more interesting and fun than dusting. It just seemed more exciting that he got to use something that had to be plugged into the wall and made so much noise.

As we compared situations, many days our frustrated response welled up into the cry, 'It's not fair!' I know we said it often enough, because I remember hearing many times my mother's succinct and apt reply, 'Life's not fair.' With those three simple words, she was faithful to teach us that everyone's circumstances and situations are different. Life might not always be fair, and the search for equality most likely would be a journey along a path of increasing discontentment.

Even as adults, we have all felt similar temptations come upon us. We may have been wandering through life quite content with what we were wearing, driving, or experiencing until, all of a sudden, we become aware that someone out there has something more. The blessing of our income level can turn sour the moment we hear that another friend works less and makes more. The home that seemed so wonderful two years ago begins to pale in comparison to our neighbor's new addition. We hear that a friend's husband sent flowers 'just because' and suddenly have the sinking feeling that we are missing out. While walking through the grocery store, we spot a well-dressed woman with the figure we would love to have and begin to grow discontent with our own shape and size.

The comparison trap can come upon us when we least expect it – the college dorm room, the workplace, the playground, the church nursery, the grocery store, and even the hospital waiting room. Everywhere we look, we are bombarded with the quest for more. This subtle comparison game, if allowed to ferment in our soul, can begin to take root and bloom into a life of discontentment and pain. The source of the problem is the sin of coveting – a sin that may appear inconsequential in comparison to the rest of the Ten Commandments. However, it is like the drop of water that can find its way into the tiny crack of a rock. Once it freezes, it can cause a fissure that damages the rock and splits it to the core. The subtle nature of the sin can often hide its painful consequences.

Coveting, envy, jealousy – these words strike at the core of our beings, for they move beyond the outward actions of our lives and pierce the inward affections of our hearts. The aim of this chapter is to develop a deeper understanding of coveting. In order to comprehend it thoroughly, we will discuss the concept in three ways. To begin, we will seek to gain a thorough and Biblical definition of coveting. Next, we will observe three characteristics about coveting that make it such a dangerous sin if allowed to fester in our hearts. Finally, we will explore four clear distinctions between right desires and covetous desires, so we can understand the type of desire residing in our own hearts. Our goal is not to stop our longings altogether, but to refine our desires and align them with the Lord's will for our lives.

A Definition of Coveting

In order to understand what something is, at times we must first begin with what it *is not*. Coveting *is not* simply having desires. Scripture is full of people who yearned for good things. The psalmists desired greatly as they cried out before the Lord. They longed for God's Word,[1] to do His will,[2] for His salvation,[3] for truth and for wisdom.[4] Hannah prayed and asked the Lord for a child year after year.[5] The

---

1 Psalm 119:40

2 Psalm 40:8

3 Psalm 119:174

4 Psalm 51:6; Proverbs 3:15-15

5 1 Samuel 1:7

writers of the New Testament also expressed their desires. Paul longed for the fellowship of other believers,[6] for the glory of Heaven,[7] the spiritual growth of the church[8] and the salvation of the Israelites,[9] and he encouraged his readers to eagerly desire spiritual gifts.[10] Jesus related our happiness with having good desires when he proclaimed, 'Blessed are those who hunger and thirst for righteousness, for they will be filled.'[11] Desiring greatly is not in opposition to contentment. In fact, Paul considered himself content in every and all circumstances[12], yet still was filled with longings.

Moreover, Moses speaks of *God* having right desires. While commanding the Israelites not to worship other gods, Moses warns them that 'the LORD, whose name is Jealous, is a jealous God.' (Exod. 34:14). This concept of righteous jealousy is difficult to understand in our world, which is often filled with jealousy that is centered on personal gain. However, in contrast to our usual picture of jealousy, the Lord's desire to secure the affections of His people is a right and good longing. It is the desire of a faithful and loving husband towards His bride, the church. He wants her affection because He has set His love upon her, covenanted with her, and purchased her redemption with His own blood. He knows that His people will not find satisfaction or contentment outside a faithful relationship with Himself. God's jealousy for His people is a demonstration of His longing for their best good. He wants our hearts to be full of the most life-giving type of desire,

---

6 Philippians 1:8; 1 Thessalonians 2:17; 2 Timothy 1:4

7 2 Corinthians 5:2; Philippians 1:23

8 Romans 1:11

9 Romans 10:1

10 1 Corinthians 12:31

11 Matthew 5:6

12 Philippians 4:12

summed up in the words of Asaph: 'Whom have I in heaven but you? And earth has nothing I desire besides you. My flesh and my heart may fail, but God is the strength of my heart and my portion forever.'[13] As we begin exploring this topic, we need to understand that our coveting is not simply a problem of having desires. It is a problem of not having the right desires in the right way.

In order to gain a correct understanding of what coveting actually is, we need to take a moment to observe the Biblical words that describe this type of desire. The Hebrew word for desire, *chamad*, is used in Scripture to describe right desires as well as inappropriate or covetous desires. In the positive sense, the word *chamad* is translated 'to desire, delight in or to be pleasant.'[14] For example, in Psalm 19, *chamad* is used to describe God's ordinances and precepts by stating, 'more to be desired are they than gold, even much fine gold.' It is right to desire God's precepts and long to know His Word. Similarly, the Greek word for desire, *epithumeo*, has both positive and negative uses in Scripture. *Epithumeo* is translated, 'to greatly desire to do or have something – to long for, to desire very much.'[15] Jesus himself used this term when he spoke to his disciples, saying, 'I have earnestly desired to eat this Passover with you before I suffer.'[16]

While there are positive uses for each of these Hebrew and Greek words, in most cases they are used to describe a negative, ungoverned, idolatrous, and selfish desire to possess.[17] The word most used to translate this concept of

---

13 Psalm 73:25- 26

14 R. Laird Harris, ed., *Theological Wordbook of the Old Testament* (Chicago: Moody, 1980), p. 673

15 Johannes P. Louw and Eugene A. Nida, eds., *Greek-English Lexicon of the New Testament* (New York: United Bible Societies, 1988).

16 Luke 22:15

17 Francis F. Brown, ed., *The Brown-Driver-Briggs Hebrew and English Lexicon* (Peabody, MA: Hendrickson, 1996).

misplaced envy and jealousy is 'coveting'. While God is at times described as jealous, He is never described as covetous. For this reason, as we discuss these concepts of misplaced desires or affections, most often I will use the term 'covet.' Every scriptural use of the word 'covet' describes an idolatrous or immoderate desire to possess. Thus, we can define coveting as: *an inordinate or culpable desire to possess, often that which belongs to another*. The term 'inordinate' speaks to desiring a good thing in a wrong or idolatrous manner, while the term 'culpable' speaks of desiring a wrong thing, clearly prohibited by Scripture.

SPECIFIC TYPES OF COVETING

At the end of this chapter, we will look at how to distinguish an inordinate desire from a right desire. For now, I will use the term 'covetous desire' to describe a sinful desire that has taken root in our heart. However, coveting is not the only term used to help explain our inappropriate desires. Coveting is such a problematic sin pattern that the Bible uses other words to help clarify types of wrong desires. Under the large umbrella of coveting are three specific subsets of coveting: envy, lust and greed. Envy describes a setting of our affections on that which specifically belongs to another. Lust describes coveting which is usually sexual in nature. Greed describes coveting which is primarily focused on the acquisition of money and possessions. Each of these specific types of coveting are aspects of the larger attitude that, if left unchecked, can consume our hearts and lead to lives of unsettled discontentment. A covetous heart pines away, never satisfied and always wanting more.

I live in the middle of a world right now that is filled with inordinate desire: I have a two-year-old. Like most two-year-olds, she is filled with many desires, and she is resentful when anyone possesses what she has decided she needs. As she plays with her other two-year-old friends, often she will notice a friend playing with one of her favorite toys. Rather than share well and join her friend in playing with the toy, she is more likely to snatch the toy away and say quite defiantly, 'mine.' Her heart, corrupted by the fall of Eden, is full of this desire to possess in an inordinate manner. It would be easy to consider this childish example and smile, thinking how far we have all come from snatching toys from one another. However, as I watch the way our world seems to run on the principle of always desiring more and doing anything to gain what we want, I wonder if the marketplace looks much different than the playground. While we may have matured in our ability to hide our displeasure, often our hearts are still full of resentment at what another has and we have decided we need.

Three Characteristics of Coveting

In order to gain greater clarity on this topic, I want us to examine three characteristics of coveting that make it such a dangerous sin if allowed to fester in our hearts. Hopefully, as we examine these truths, we will continue to grow in our understanding of how coveting acts as a parasite on our hearts, leaving us malnourished and robbed of the nutrients we need.

Coveting is a sin pattern, not a circumstance

As we seek to understand what coveting entails, it is important to recognize that it is a sin pattern of our hearts, not a set of circumstances we are facing. Coveting can so blind our minds that we come to believe that if we could just attain the longed for item (a job, a baby, a spouse, healing), then we would be able to be content in life. However, our inordinate desires are never solved by attainment. Today we may covet one item, but once it is given, we will soon begin to desire something else.

In fact, rather than quenching the fire of coveting, often attaining an item gives us a greater desire to possess more. The more we have, the more we want. A reporter once asked

Nelson Rockefeller, 'How much money does it take to be happy?' He replied, 'Just a little bit more.' The sin of coveting eats away at our hearts and is insatiable in its appetite. Our greatest malady is not our set of circumstances, but the blindness and hardness that overtakes our hearts. We spend our time, resources and energies all in an attempt to gain more and then once the item is attained we soon will find ourselves chasing the next desire in an inappropriate manner. It is a pattern that works in our hearts, and it always leaves us empty.

Solomon, the wealthiest and wisest king in Israel's history, looked back over his life and lamented, 'I denied myself nothing my eyes desired; I refused my heart no pleasure. My heart took delight in all my work, and this was the reward for all my labor. Yet when I surveyed all that my hands had done and what I had toiled to achieve, everything was meaningless, a chasing after the wind; nothing was gained under the sun.'[18] Solomon realized that gaining all the pleasures and riches of this world did not satisfy his soul.

In contrast, God invites us to come to His table saying, 'Listen, listen to me, and eat what is good, and your soul will delight in the richest of fare.'[19] Our difficult circumstances and places of longing are not cause to covet, but are God's invitation to come and find life in Him alone. If we want to avoid the regret of Solomon, we must accept that our covetous desires arise because of our sin, not our situations. Gaining all the world has to offer will be meaningless if our hearts fail to find satisfaction in the Lord.

I experienced the reality of this heart problem when my husband and I lived overseas in Edinburgh, Scotland for a couple of years while he worked on his Ph.D. The initial move was a difficult one for me. In our first (and very tiny) flat, we lived without some of our American niceties.

---

18 Ecclesiastes 2:10-11

19 Isaiah 55:2

Our washer and dryer were located three floors down in a shared space. Our only transportation was the bus or our feet since we were without a car. Our dorm-size refrigerator required multiple shopping trips per week, and the lack of a dishwasher made for a much longer clean-up after dinner. More importantly, I was often lonely, missing dear friends and family. It was painful to consider that they were all still sharing life together, while I was alone in a new place. I spent many early days there coveting items that had over time become expectations in my heart. Quietly, I would say to myself, 'Well, I'd be a lot more joyful if I wasn't so exhausted from walking everywhere.' Or complain inwardly, 'Laundry wouldn't be so difficult if I didn't have to haul it down all these stairs and then wait to put it in the dryer.' On evenings alone, I would sit and wonder what my friends were doing, believing that they must all be having so much fun just being together.

Now that I am back living in the States, I drive everywhere instead of walking. Often, I find myself tired of being in the car shuttling my children to and fro. Currently, I own my own washer and dryer. In fact, I have a laundry room. Our life is full of friends, family and social activities. Have these favorable changes of circumstances made me a more joyful and contented person? No, these favorable circumstances have not led to my personal satisfaction. Changes of circumstances can lead to temporary delight, but without God's grace at work, my desire for my own washer and dryer can quickly turn into the new covetous thought, 'Wouldn't it be nice if I had a maid to do all this laundry for me?' My problem was never about where my washer and dryer were located or whether or not we owned a car. My problem was in accepting the Lord's will for my life, which involved these very trivial items that I grumbled and complained about in my heart. I can say that by God's grace He is changing my heart to trust and rejoice in him, regardless of my circumstances. However, my heart is the thing that needs changing, not my circumstances. If my heart is not freed from this sin pattern, then I will go from initial coveting to more coveting, with attainment gaining me only temporary happiness.

I know that the example I share focuses on the relatively mundane areas of life. Many of you are dealing with much deeper, heart-felt longings. Some of the things you are longing for seem to be the gateway to all your other longings. However, coveting often takes hold in these everyday areas of our lives. Disappointments fester in our hearts and grumbling and complaining become our habit. As thankfulness decreases, we find ourselves increasingly discontent, regardless of the significance of our struggle. Any type of covetous desire, from the insignificant to the complex, is an offense before God. Therefore, as we unpack coveting, the first thing to grasp is that it is an inward sin pattern, not an outward circumstance.

Coveting is marked by comparison and entitlement

The second characteristic we need to understand about coveting is that it is marked by comparison with and entitlement towards our neighbor and his possessions. If you are wondering where in your own life you are coveting, consider where you compare your life with others the most. Coveting is all about looking over the fence into another's life and desiring what that person has as we compare their circumstances with our own situation. It is not just a neutral observation: 'Oh, that is a great house'. Instead, it is an entitled, accusing desire: 'That is a great house. I should have a house like that. Why doesn't God give me a house like that? Why does God always seem to be blessing everyone but me?'

The tenth commandment warns us against this type of comparison and entitlement. Deuteronomy 5:21 states, 'You shall not covet your neighbor's wife. You shall not set your desire on your neighbor's house or land, his manservant or maidservant, his ox or donkey, or anything that belongs to your neighbor.' It is most easy to covet that which is closest to us because that is where we begin the comparison game. As we play this dangerous game, we find ourselves determining exactly the kind of life that would be best. We would like one neighbor's perfect home, another's loving marriage, another's income level and another's helpful in-laws that always seem to be there at a moment's notice. We begin by considering how much easier or better our life would be with the attainment of these items and slowly a sense of entitlement grows in our hearts.

The covetous desire speaks the following lie: 'If God blesses any other woman in any way, then I have a right to that blessing as well.' This type of picking and choosing is a kind of blindness. Perhaps our neighbor does have a wonderful home, but her marriage is falling apart. Perhaps the friend's income comes at a great cost of working long hours and time away from family and friends. In every life, there are blessings and hardships. Coveting blinds us to the hardships of our neighbor and instead focuses in on the ways the Lord is blessing her with what we desire. Her hardships will seem light in your eyes – how can she have any significant struggle when she has the one thing you desire? Coveting is the antithesis of Christ's command to 'love your neighbor as yourself,'[20] because our neighbor becomes our enemy simply by possessing what we desire. We cannot love well those whose lives or belongings we covet.

To further help us understand how coveting is marked by comparison and entitlement, it is useful to study the writings of church leaders throughout time and gain wisdom from their insight. The Westminster Standards are a set of documents that were established in 1649 by men appointed by the British Parliament to study the Scriptures. The Westminster Catechism is a section of the Standards and is a wonderful document that uses a question and answer

20 Mark 12:31

format discussing various truths of the faith. It delves into each of the Ten Commandments with two questions: 'What are the sins forbidden in this commandment?' and 'What are the duties required of this commandment?' The response of the Westminster Catechism to the question of the sins forbidden in the commandment, 'Do not covet', is as follows:

> Question 148: What are the sins forbidden in the tenth commandment?
>
> Answer: The sins forbidden in the tenth commandment are, discontentment with our own estate; envying and grieving at the good of our neighbor, together with all inordinate motions and affections to anything that is his.

The Westminster Catechism describes three primary ways coveting expresses itself within our hearts. The first indication of coveting is discontentment with our own estate. Our dissatisfaction may grow because we compare our life with those around us, or because our present reality is quite different from our own personal hopes, dreams and expectations of life. Whatever the cause, discontentment is a sure sign that our heart is coveting something in an inordinate manner.

Secondly, the Catechism points out that if you are envying or grieving the good of your neighbor, you are coveting. If you find out about a good circumstance that has happened to your neighbor – an excellent test score, a fun experience, a positive medical diagnosis, a new job, a new possession of some sort, a proposal of marriage, a pregnancy, a ministry success, a long-sought answer to prayer – and your response is envy or grief at their good circumstance, you can be assured that you are struggling with the tenth commandment. Truly, our envy or grief at another's good shows forth the ugliness of this sin in our hearts. Our ability to 'rejoice with those who rejoice' is consumed by our own dissatisfaction with life. We find God's goodness to others a cause for grief because we wrongly believe that God has failed to be good to us. In this great failure to trust God, we rob both neighbor and ourselves the pleasure of sharing in joy.

Lastly, the Catechism speaks of having inordinate motions and affections towards anything that belongs to your neighbor. If you set your desires or affections on what belongs to your neighbor, you will never be able to love that person well. You will think of them only in terms of what they possess instead of who they are. It is important to clarify at this point that these affections are not just towards physical possessions. The Catechism speaks well in saying that we are wrong to set our affections on *anything* that belongs to our neighbor. This includes their physical possessions, but it is not limited to them. When I was up many long nights with a newborn, I used to truly covet sleep. I would look at friends who were sleeping through the night every night and wonder how they could complain about anything, because every night they were blessed with the wonderful possession of sleep. We long for different things at different points in our lives. We covet experiences, possessions, emotional resources, educational levels, obedient children, marriages, life stages, giftedness, intellectual abilities, and a myriad of things much more than just our neighbor's new cute coat. To limit it to physical possessions greatly minimizes the tenth commandment and fails to get to the heart of our situation.

God wants contentment in all things regarding our own estate because He is the Lord of all of our circumstances. From that deep contentment will flow a right desire for and rejoicing at the good of our neighbor. In contrast, our coveting is marked by an entitled comparison that leads to resentment towards God and isolation from true community with others.

Coveting is a begetting sin

The last characteristic to help us understand the seriousness of coveting is the notion that it is a sin that begets other sins. Thomas Watson called covetousness a 'mother sin' because it leads us to break each of the Ten Commandments.[21] He explains that coveting leads us to break the first commandment because the object of our desire becomes another god that we worship and love. We break the fourth commandment to obey the Sabbath because our covetous desires lead us to spend our time on our own pleasures instead of the worship of God. Adultery begins first with the covetous desire of lust. Stealing begins with envy of that which belongs to another. Our covetous desires do not simply stay in the inner reaches of our hearts. James tells us, 'But each one is tempted when, by his own evil desire, he is dragged away and enticed. Then, after desire has conceived, it gives birth to sin; and sin, when it is full-grown, gives birth to death.'[22] As we contemplate these wrong desires and set our hearts upon them, they will give birth to outward sins that will eventually lead to death. We need to take seriously the effect that these inner desires have on our physical, emotional and spiritual life. If left unchecked, they eventually will lead to great sorrow and consequences in our own lives and the lives of those around us.

We will spend the second half of this book unpacking the many ways coveting draws us into harming others and the pattern it usually takes in our life. However, here at the start, I would like to give some examples of ways our desires can become filled with resentment and lead us to act

21 Thomas Watson, *The Ten Commandments* (Edinburgh: The Banner of Truth Trust, 1965), p. 177.

22 James 1:14-15

in culpable ways towards others. As you read, observe the subtle nature of the sin and the harm that can result as inward desires beget outward actions.

Examples of Coveting

Picture two ten-year-old girls discussing their summer plans. Amy joyfully describes the month-long camp she attends with swimming, horseback riding, soccer, water skiing and sailing. As Mary listens to Amy, her plans of going to the library and reading books in addition to a week-long camp in town begin to sound increasingly boring. Mary begins to feel sorry for herself, and in an attempt to hide her feelings, she tells Amy that she would hate to go to summer camp for an entire month. 'Wouldn't there be bugs? Isn't it hot out in the sun everyday? I'm so thankful my parents don't make me go to camp for an entire month.' Mary's comments fizzle Amy's excitement, and she leaves the conversation discouraged and nervous about going to camp.

Two college roommates are taking the same class. Jennifer quickly absorbs information from class lectures and easily completes the reading assignments. Susan struggles to pay attention and finds her mind wandering every time she tries to get through the reading materials. On the day before the test, Jennifer studies for an hour or two and then joins some friends for dinner and a fun night of hanging out. She asks Susan to join them, but Susan declines, knowing she needs to study. When the exams are returned Susan is excited that she received a B until she learns that Jennifer made an A. When Jennifer invites her to dinner to celebrate exams being finished, in her frustration, Susan rejects the offer. Instead, she phones a friend to vent her disappointment. Throughout the conversation she subtly makes unkind remarks about Jennifer that leave her feeling hollow and guilt-ridden.

Two girlfriends have known each other since middle school. Sharon got married a few years ago, while Anne is still in the singles group at church, hoping to meet someone. They used to talk all the time, share clothes, go running, but now a coldness has grown between them. Sharon dreads having to tell Anne that she is pregnant (even though she is thankful to be pregnant after two difficult years of trying). She knows that her happiness will most likely be hurtful to Anne who feels like she is stuck in the same life stage. Anne feels like everyone else's life continues to go on and progress, while hers consists of having to attend shower after shower to celebrate other people's joy.

Two women are neighbors and members of the same church. Both ladies have small children at home. Elizabeth's husband comes home every night for dinner with the kids. Margaret's husband works late most evenings and gets home just in time to help put the kids to bed. Margaret's usual day turns more difficult as both her children get the stomach bug and her husband calls to let her know that he will be later than usual this evening. When he finally does come home, exhausted after a long day of work, Margaret meets him with coldness and anger. Rather than rest together after a long day for both of them, they turn on each other and use their remaining energy fighting. Margaret says to herself, 'My marriage would be so different if my husband could come home earlier like Elizabeth's'.

As each year passes, Catherine laments the fact that her body continues to show the signs of aging. Her clothes feel tighter, her skin grows wrinkled, and her hair changes both in color and texture. She looks at women younger than herself and wants to once again feel beautiful. Actually, she'd be glad to just look a little more like her former self. With each passing year she spends increasing amounts of time and money to find new outfits, creams, exercises and surgeries to feed her desire for beauty. While her desire represents a right longing, the depth of her desire overflows into increasing discontentment and comparison with other women. Her continual pursuit of outer beauty leaves her empty and dissatisfied on the inside.

Two ladies both live in the same retirement home. Each day all of the members come and eat together in the cafeteria. Evelyn has family still living in town and they often come to take her to visit the doctor, sit with her and talk, or take her out for dinner. Janet longs to see her grandchildren, but they all live far away and rarely take the time to write. Evelyn invites Janet to join her family for Thanksgiving dinner, but Janet declines. Rather than attempt to get to know anyone at this stage of life, she decides it would be best to just be alone.

In all of these examples, the women set their affections on what belonged to another person. From our early years to our golden years, we covet experiences, intelligence, giftedness, time, help, financial resources, relationships, life stages and physical health. Each of these women compared their lot to the lot of another and felt they came up short. Once they compared what they had to another, their personal discontentment led them to make harmful choices. Coveting begets outward sin that affects both the good of our neighbor and our own good. In our desire to possess, we come to find ourselves enslaved to a pattern that keeps us from experiencing joy and contentment.

Distinguishing Between Desires

At this point, you may be asking a good question: 'How do I distinguish between right desires and inordinate or culpable desires in my own life?' To close this chapter, we will observe four clear distinctions between longing well and coveting. Hopefully, the contrast between the two will help summarize and clarify what we have discussed thus far. As we begin, let me say that this question penetrates the heart and is not easily answered. Some days, we desire rightly, trusting the Lord in our places of waiting. Other days, we grumble and complain and are full of a covetous spirit. We live in a sinful, fallen world. We were created for Eden and a part of us will always long for all things to be made right. The reality of life is that each one of us will face disappointments that cause us to ask, 'Why?' Why is the Lord not giving me a husband? Why do I have to live in this city? Why am I unable to get pregnant? Why can my husband still not find a job? Why did the Lord not heal my mother? Why do my children not obey? Why does no one seem to notice or care about me?

As we wait for a new, redeemed world entrusting our circumstances to the Lord prevents bitterness from hardening our hearts. How we handle the disappointing 'whys' of our lives affords us great insight into the health of our longings. The following four heart checks help us to know if our desire for something has grown immoderate or culpable:

1. The object of our desire is wrong.
2. The means to go about obtaining our desire is wrong.
3. The motivation for our desire is wrong.
4. The attitude while waiting for our desire is wrong.

The object is wrong

The first heart check to distinguish between an upright desire and an inordinate desire is to determine if the object of our desire is wrong. If what we are longing for is against the will of the Lord as revealed in the Scriptures, then we can know for certain that we are coveting. For instance, if you are longing after someone else's spouse, you are clearly coveting, for the Bible tells us that adultery is wrong. If you long to repay evil to someone who has hurt you, then this longing is wrong, for Christ commands, 'Love your enemies, do good to those who hate you, bless those who curse you, pray for those who mistreat you.'[23] If the object of our longings is outside God's will, we need to let go of those desires or we are coveting in our hearts.

A clear Scriptural example of this culpable desire for a wrong object is from our first mother, Eve. While we will study her example and the pattern of her sin in greater depth in later chapters, I think it is helpful to note that the first of all sins began with a covetous desire. She saw that the fruit was desirable and ignored the Lord's command not to eat from the tree of good and evil. She set her heart on that which was clearly outside of God's will for her life. Thus, her desire was clearly culpable because the object of her longing was against the Lord's good command. She showed forth her distrust of His goodness and took the fruit and ate of it. Thus, the first sin of disobedience began with coveting and led to every sin that ever has been. Coveting, the sin that seems so inward and harmless, led Eve on a path of death and destruction, while all the time promising the gift of life. A mistaken desire for any object that is outside of God's revealed will is clearly covetous in nature.

The means is wrong

The second heart check on our desires deals with the means we are willing to use in order to get what we want. If we are willing to use inappropriate means to gain what we desire, then our desire has become inordinate. In this case, the object of our desires may be right, but willingness to compromise God's Word and use incorrect means to gain what we desire shows forth our covetous heart. For instance, if a woman longs to have a welcoming, hospitable home, that is a good and right end. However, if she goes into great debt to obtain all of the furnishings she believes she needs to make her home hospitable, then she is actually coveting. She has used a good end (a welcoming home)

---

23 Luke 6:27

to justify a wrong means (going into unnecessary debt). Another example of this principle would be the right desire of a single woman for a husband. It is a good thing to desire a companion and mate. However, if she is willing to dress immodestly or spend her time unwisely in order to attract a mate, then her means is outside of God's will and shows forth a covetous heart.

A scriptural example of this second principle is found by looking at Sarah's example in Genesis 16. One chapter earlier, God met with Abram and covenanted with him, promising that his descendants would be as many as the stars in the heavens. Sarah had a right and good desire for a child. In fact, she even had a promise that God would give Abram numerous descendants. Her end was clearly one that God had promised and would bring to fruition. However, instead of waiting patiently for God to accomplish what He had promised, Sarah took charge and used an incorrect means to accomplish her desire for a family. She took her maidservant Hagar and gave her to Abram to produce a child. Hagar did conceive, and this led to her hatred of Sarah and eventually Sarah's abuse of Hagar. Sarah's willingness to use wrong means to bring about a good end shows forth her covetous heart. A heart that is longing well can wait for God to accomplish His promises. It is a waiting full of trust that does not lean on its own understanding. In contrast, a covetous heart schemes and plots, using human wisdom to accomplish desired goals and outcomes.

The motivation is wrong

The third heart check deals with the reasons that we have a particular desire in the first place. If our motivation for wanting something is marked or sparked by comparison with other people, then we can assume we are coveting. Usually, this third heart check brings to light most of our coveting. Consider why you want the clothing, home, marriage, job or vacation you desire. Often our very desires begin because we find out another couple took a lovely trip to the Caribbean or found a great home in a particular neighborhood. Perhaps all of our friends are attempting to get their children into just the right school or begin working at the same company. If we are using other people to determine what we desire out of life, then we are not listening to God's direction and plan for our own life. Instead of following God, we are similar to our old middle-school self and still just following the crowd. On this path of borrowed longings we will find ourselves continually empty and always coming up short. Even as we gain these items, we come to realize that they do not fulfill our lives, because they were not true longings of our own heart; they are just things we came to believe we should have because our neighbor possessed them.

A Biblical example of this principle can be seen in the Israelites' response to Samuel at the end of his life. The Israelites decided that they wanted a king to rule them, not because it was God's will or His timing, but because they told Samuel, 'appoint a king to lead us, such as all the other nations have.'[24] Their desire for a king was because the nations around them had a king. Samuel tells them that a king will take their sons and daughters into his service, take the best fruits of their fields and vineyards, and take the best of their cattle, donkeys and servants for his own use. Eventually, Samuel warns them, they will cry out for relief from the king they chose for themselves. In spite of all they will lose, the Israelites cling to their covetous desire for a king because they believe he will make them great like all the other nations. When our desires begin because we compare our lives to those around us, and not because of God's work in our life, we can be assured that we are

24 1 Samuel 8:5

coveting items that will only lead us to cry out for relief from the very items we desired.

Our attitude is wrong

The last heart check on our longings comes as we look at the attitude we have as we wait for God to bring about what we desire. If our attitude while we wait is full of complaining, bitterness, anger or unthankfulness, then we are coveting. We desire rightly when we can wait on God to provide the longings of our heart with joy and thankfulness at what He has already given us. Paul encouraged this response when he wrote, 'Be joyful always, pray continually; give thanks in all circumstances, for this is God's will for you in Christ Jesus.'[25]

One day a few years ago, some friends and I were at the park with our children. We usually meet to play at a fenced park that has slides, swings and a fun sandbox for the children to use and enjoy. Just next to the playground is a field where we sometimes let the older children run and play. However, it is next to a road, and since there are often young children in the mix, many times we have to limit our play to the fenced-in areas. One day the older children asked to be allowed to play outside of the fence. All of the moms agreed that it was not a good idea, so we told them 'no, today we are just going to play in the playground area.' Rather than play and enjoy all that was given to them – slides, swings, and a large sandbox, each of the children chose to stand at the fence and just look at the field. They missed all that had been given to them because they were so busy longing for what was denied. They chose to complain and be miserable about what they were not allowed to do, instead of enjoying a park full of things specifically designed for their amusement. So often in our seasons of waiting, we miss out on all that the Lord

---

25 1 Thessalonians 5:16 -18

has given us because we are consumed coveting the item or situation we think we need.

The Israelites' wandering and waiting in the desert provides a similar example of this principle. Just two months after experiencing a miraculous redemption from slavery, the Israelites grumbled and complained against Aaron and Moses: 'If only we had died by the LORD's hand in Egypt! There we sat around pots of meat and ate all the food we wanted, but you have brought us out into this desert to starve this entire assembly to death.'[26] The manna of the Lord was not enough for the Israelites. All they could think about was the meat they used to enjoy in Egypt. They were willing to return to the land of their slavery, rather than be denied what they believed they needed. Their unwillingness to be thankful for the daily provisions of God clearly demonstrated their great distrust of the Lord. Their unthankful and complaining hearts showed forth their envious and inordinate desires. In contrast, a heart that is content can wait patiently for what is lacking, bearing fruit in every season. The Apostle Paul tells us that the fruit of God's Spirit is 'love, joy, peace, patience, kindness, goodness, faithfulness, gentleness and self-control.'[27] One who has learned to trust in the Father's goodness can bear such fruit in any and every circumstance.

As we conclude this chapter, it is helpful to note that the areas where we lack joy and thankfulness or find ourselves angry and full of grumbling are most likely the areas in which we are coveting. It would be easy to just attempt to change our attitude, thinking, 'I'm going to grumble and complain less, so then I won't be coveting.' However, our attitude is merely the fruit of the reality that is living inside our heart. It will not be enough to simply change our outward behavior; we need our hearts

---

26 Exodus 16:3

27 Galatians 5:22

to be changed. A heart that is full of disquiet and distrust will not be easily fixed by attempting to complain less or by putting a positive spin on our struggles. In the next chapter, we will look in-depth at the root causes of coveting and unpack the unbelief that leads to our inordinate desires. We will look deep into the character of God and discover that our understanding of who He is greatly affects our ability to live a life of contentment and joy. Our core problem in coveting is not our attitude or the circumstances we find ourselves in; our core problem is our unbelief in some characteristic of God. Hopefully, as we look in detail at all that Christ has done, our faith will grow, and our belief in God will lead us to put on new desires. All other possessions and relationships that promise life are simply broken cisterns that eventually run dry. Abundant life is found in Christ alone.

Questions for Personal Reflection and Group Discussion

Dealing with the sin of coveting begins with identifying it in our lives. While later chapters will give more detail about ways to address this sin, an important first step is to reflect on how this pattern manifests itself in our day-to-day lives. These questions are designed to help you think more specifically about the nature and the presence of coveting.

1. When we look at our world, how does it encourage the desire and pursuit for more? Can you think of advertisements, TV shows or people in your life that seem to embody the notion that more is better?
2. The definition given for coveting was: '*an inordinate or culpable desire to possess, often that which belongs to another*'. What is meant by the term inordinate? What is meant by the term culpable? What are some examples of inordinate desires? Culpable desires?

3. What are some examples of good things we should desire? Thinking through both the chapter and your own knowledge of the Bible, what are some things that God desires?
4. Read Ecclesiastes 2:10-11. What was Solomon's experience with life? Why do you think at the end of his life he experienced a prevailing emptiness? How does this compare to God's invitation in Isaiah 55:1-3?
5. Have you experienced the reality of coveting being 'a sin pattern and not a circumstance'? How have you seen covetous desires remain, in spite of changes in circumstances? Think through what you desired as a child, college student, in your mid-twenties, mid-thirties and so on. How have you struggled with these desires in every season of life?
6. Read Deuteronomy 5:21. How does coveting prevent us from loving our neighbor well?
7. The Westminster Catechism asks:

   Question 148: What are the sins forbidden in the tenth commandment?

   Answer: The sins forbidden in the tenth commandment are, discontentment with our own estate; envying and grieving at the good of our neighbor, together with all inordinate motions and affections to anything that is his.

   How does this answer expand your understanding of coveting? What part of this answer do you find the most convicting?

8. Read James 1:14-15. Think through your life, the world around you, and examples in the Bible. How have you seen the reality that coveting is a 'begetting sin'? How does sin tend to progress and give birth to more sin?

9. In the chapter, there was a description of small children looking over the fence at a grassy field, complaining that they weren't allowed to play there. All the while, they were missing the entire playground that was built for their enjoyment. Can you think of times in your life that you missed the joys of a season because you were so preoccupied by what you wanted?

10. At the end of the chapter, four heart checks were given to help us understand if our desires have grown inordinate or culpable. Can you think of some examples when:

    a. The object of your desire was wrong?

    b. You used wrong means to obtain your desire?

    c. The motivation for your desire was wrong?

    d. Your attitude while waiting was wrong?

11. Which one of these 'heart checks' exposes the place you are currently coveting? What item are you longing for in an immoderate or culpable manner today?

12. Read Titus 3:3-8. As you consider these verses, what encouragement do you find in them regarding the love and kindness of Christ? How does His mercy and grace encourage you as you consider the sin of coveting?

2 *The Root of Coveting*

We can now see how the pardon of sin, an interest in Christ, a sense of God's love, and the assurance of glory, are the only indispensables. Christ alone is the one thing necessary, and all others are but 'maybes' at best. All the world has is but loss and dung in comparison with the excellence of the knowledge of Jesus Christ our Lord. Without him the soul is undone to all eternity.

THOMAS CASE

Voices From the Past, p. 173.

2

The Root of Coveting:

Unbelief

It is easier to unpack and understand the definition of a sin pattern like coveting than it is to understand why we fall into these same patterns time and time again. Often we experience disappointment in ourselves, as well as the negative impact on others, and inwardly we decide to try harder to fight our covetous desires. We want to remove our tendency towards envy, lust and greed, yet as soon as one covetous weed is removed, another seems to sprout in a new area of our heart. Our inability to fight well and conquer this sin is related to our attempt to treat only the outer symptoms of what is a much deeper, inner problem. The aim of this chapter is to get to the heart of our coveting. We have looked at what it is; now we will consider why we return to the same unfulfilling pattern of behavior. If our pursuit of earthly gain leaves us empty, why do we continue to run after these temporal pleasures? Our core problem is not the outward fruit of our sin, but our inner unbelief. Essentially, all coveting (and all sin for that matter) is rooted in unbelief.

In this chapter we will focus on three particular areas of unbelief that cause us to fall into covetous patterns. We will spend the majority of our time contemplating what the Bible reveals about God and how our failure to believe and trust in His character is at the core of our coveting. Our lack of contentment primarily flows from unbelief regarding God's sovereignty and goodness in our lives. Secondly, we will examine the true calling of a Christian and how our coveting is both a rejection of that calling and rebellion against our true purpose. Lastly, we will unpack the Bible's call on our relationships with our neighbor and how our incorrect understanding of our neighbor leads to disunity and discord within the body of Christ. This triumvirate of unbelief – towards God, our purpose and our neighbor – produces our covetous desires. As we take off our unbelief, we must put on truth in order to guard our minds in Christ.

THE GREAT OFFENSE: UNBELIEF IN THE CHARACTER OF GOD

As we start this chapter, it might be easy to question the need to study the character of God. How exactly does understanding His character relate to our discontentment? Let me start with an example. Picture a young child asking for a treat at snack time. The mother, in her wisdom, knows that too many treats are not healthy for her child. She tells her child 'no' and offers her an apple instead. The child does not understand that her mother's actions towards her are for her own good. Instead, she throws a tantrum and is forced to go to her room until she calms down. The child's covetousness flows from a lack of understanding and belief in her mother's goodness towards her. It also is the result of a lack of understanding of how her own body works best. She believes that what tastes good will make her happy. The mother, who has correct understanding, knows that too many treats will actually keep her body from working well and in the end will lead to greater discontentment. As the child comes to maturity and grows into an adult, her understanding will lead her to thankfulness at her mother's care and discipline.

In a similar way, it is important for us to understand God's character in new and deeper ways if we want to live thankful, contented lives. In understanding God and His good purpose for our lives, we can fight our temptation to think we know the best plan for our lives. Just as a mature child can sit at the table and receive with thanksgiving whatever food her loving mother gives her, so a mature Christian can receive the circumstances and plans given to her for each day from her sovereign and loving Father. However, our ability to be thankful and content in all things is directly related to our understanding of God's character. We need to understand the extent of both His goodness and His sovereignty if we are to rejoice in His daily provision for our lives.

We also must understand that our coveting is not just a quiet, inward sin that robs us of contentment and joy. It is actually an assault of unbelief that is of great offense to God's name and character. In fact, in Colossians 3:5, Paul equates covetousness with idolatry. In a sermon on this passage, John Piper thoughtfully inquires, 'Have you ever considered that the Ten Commandments begin and end with virtually the same commandment? "You shall have no other gods before me" (Exod. 20:3) and "You shall not covet" (Exod. 20:17) are almost equivalent commands. Coveting is desiring anything other than God in a way that betrays a loss of contentment and satisfaction in him. Covetousness is a heart divided between two gods. So Paul calls it idolatry.'[1]

A covetous heart reveals that our affections have turned from the one true God to the vain and false idols that we worship. Essentially, our unbelief begets our covetousness, and our covetousness gives birth to our idolatry. We fail to love the Lord and glorify Him with our lives because we believe that life is found in the object of our desire instead of the Giver of all good and perfect gifts. Ultimately, our idolatry flows out of deep unbelief in two primary components of

1 By John Piper. © *Desiring God*. Website: desiringGod.org October 30, 1988.

God's character. Our covetousness and discontentment emanate primarily from a mistrust of God's *sovereignty* and *goodness*. Exploring these two traits thoroughly will help us escape our unbelief and increase our worship of God alone. In order to do so, we will study the extent of God's sovereignty and goodness as described in the Bible, as well as the wisdom passed down throughout the history of the church through insightful creeds and confessions.

THE SOVEREIGNTY OF GOD

Understanding the magnitude of God's sovereignty is a good place to begin. Let me say up front, this concept is multifaceted, and numerous books have been written defending God's sovereignty in much greater detail than we will achieve in this chapter. For our purposes, I simply want us to look at some Biblical passages that highlight God's reign over our lives. His sovereignty extends over life, death, illness, salvation, creation, suffering, sin, and every circumstance that comes into our life. He not only knows the number of hairs on our head; he ordained exactly how many would be there.

Lord over all our days

In Psalm 139, David speaks with amazement at the magnitude of God's providence. He states, 'You know when I sit and when I rise; you perceive my thoughts from afar. You discern my going out and my lying down; you are familiar with all my ways. Before a word is on my tongue you know it completely, O LORD. You hem me in – behind and before; you have laid your hand upon me.' He continues to express the depth of God's dominion by proclaiming, 'All the days ordained for me were written in your book before one of them came to be.' David exults in a God that reigns from above in such a way that He is Lord over both life and death, as well as the smaller details of a person's daily comings and goings. He also admits that this knowledge of God is too wonderful for him, too lofty to attain. The notion that God ordains all of our days is complex. Our finite brains can only begin to comprehend an infinite being, completely set apart in nature from ourselves.

Lord over our salvation

God's sovereignty continues over another extremely important area in our life – our salvation. In Ephesians 1:3-6, Paul rejoices, 'Praise be to the God and Father of our Lord Jesus Christ, who has blessed us in the heavenly realms with every spiritual blessing in Christ. For he chose us in him before the creation of the world to be holy and blameless in his sight. In love he predestined us to be adopted as his sons through Jesus Christ, in accordance with his pleasure and will – to the praise of his glorious grace, which he has freely given us in the One he loves.' He asserts a similar truth to the Romans when he recalls God's words to Moses, 'I will have mercy on whom I have mercy, and I will have compassion on whom I have compassion.'[2] Our salvation does not depend on our own desire or effort, but rests fully on the mercy of God. In our sinful state, we were so lost that we did not have the ability to believe in God, unless His Spirit awakened our hearts to the good news of the gospel. A heart softened by the Spirit can respond to the Word preached. However, a heart hardened by sin's deceitfulness will only grow harder still upon hearing the tidings of God. Only God's Spirit can awaken a heart to believe the message of sin and redemption. The scriptures clearly assert that God's salvation was planned for His people before the creation of the world. His sovereignty extends over all who will come to believe in His name.

Lord over suffering and sin

God's sovereignty also encompasses the suffering and sin that comes into or flows out of our lives. The story of Joseph in the book of Genesis illustrates God's sovereignty over man's sinful choices, while still upholding man's responsibility for

2 Romans 9:15

the choices he makes. Joseph's brothers were jealous because Joseph was his father's favorite. Their evil desires led them to sell their brother into slavery, while reporting to their father, Jacob, that wild animals had killed him. Joseph experiences many hardships in the land of Egypt, often as a result of other people's sinful behaviors. At the end of the story, Joseph's brothers come to Egypt to escape the famine that has devastated their land. Joseph invites them to return with their father Jacob and live with the Egyptians. After Jacob dies, the brothers fear that Joseph will now exact his revenge. Instead, Joseph comforts his brothers with these words, 'Do not fear, for am I in the place of God? As for you, you meant evil against me, but God meant it for good, to bring it about that many people should be kept alive, as they are today.'[3] Notice that Joseph asserts two seemingly incompatible truths – his brothers intended to work evil, but God intended to work good. This statement essentially shows forth the mystery of God's sovereignty. God fully rules over even the evil intents of His subjects, yet man is fully responsible for the evil acts he commits. God's rule over man's choices does not negate the fact that man makes sinful choices and rebels against God's call. The Belgic Confession explains this mystery in the following way:

> We believe that the same God, after he had created all things, did not forsake them, or give them up to fortune or chance, but that he rules and governs them according to his holy will, so that nothing happens in this world without his appointment: nevertheless, God neither is the author of, nor can be charged with, the sins which are committed. For his power and goodness are so great and incomprehensible, that he orders and executes his work in the most excellent and just manner, even then, when devils and wicked men act unjustly. And, as to what he doth surpassing human understanding, we will not curiously inquire into, farther than our capacity will admit of; but with the greatest

3 Genesis 50:19 -20 ESV.

> humility and reverence adore the righteous judgments of God, which are hid from us, contenting ourselves that we are disciples of Christ, to learn only those things which he has revealed to us in his Word, without transgressing these limits. This doctrine affords us unspeakable consolation, since we are taught thereby that nothing can befall us by chance, but by the direction of our most gracious and heavenly Father; who watches over us with a paternal care, keeping all creatures so under his power, that not a hair of our head (for they are all numbered), nor a sparrow, can fall to the ground, without the will of our Father, in whom we do entirely trust; being persuaded, that he so restrains the devil and all our enemies, that without his will and permission, they cannot hurt us.[4]

Thus, all circumstances that come into our lives flow from His providence. This description of God's sovereignty may not answer all of our questions, but it does point us to the wonderful consolation that is found in this doctrine. All the circumstances that happen in our lives are planned and ordained from the Lord. His Providence extends from the family we were given to the traffic we faced on the way to work this morning. However, the doctrine of God's sovereignty only brings us comfort if it is linked with a second character trait – His goodness.

The Goodness of God

By the goodness of the Lord, I am referring to God's love, kindness, mercy, grace, righteousness, justice and holiness. The notion that God is providentially reigning over all events only brings comfort if it is linked to the fact that He is ruling all things in a loving and just manner. In Romans 8, Paul reminds his readers, 'And we know that in all things God works for the good of those who love Him, who have been called according to His purpose.'[5] In all things – from the major events of your

4 Belgic Confession, Article 13 – Of Divine Providence.

5 Romans 8:28

life, to the seemingly insignificant – God is at work for your good. This is truly an amazing statement, and it demonstrates God's active providence and goodness towards His children. In addition, the Old Testament Psalms rejoice by saying, 'Give thanks to the LORD, for he is good; his love endures forever.'[6] The Psalmist's thankfulness flowed out in response to God's goodness and love. When God appeared to Moses on Mt. Sinai, He proclaimed Himself to be, 'The LORD, the LORD, the compassionate and gracious God, slow to anger, abounding in love and faithfulness, maintaining love to thousands, and forgiving wickedness, rebellion and sin.'[7] Essentially, God declares Himself (and all of His actions) to be good.

God's goodness and sovereignty are shown in greatest detail at the cross of Christ. There is no greater demonstration of His righteousness, goodness, mercy, love and sovereignty than at the cross. Speaking at Pentecost, Peter declares, 'This man was handed over to you by God's set purpose and foreknowledge; and you, with the help of wicked men, put him to death by nailing him to the cross.'[8] The cross of Christ was not a random act of violence that God worked for good. Paul asserts it was a providentially planned event, ordained by God's set purpose, that He worked for good. The most evil event that has ever occurred in human history happened in accordance with God's set purpose. However, also notice that it was man's wickedness that put Christ to death on the cross. Here again we see the mystery of God's purpose working for good in all that happens, but man's responsibility for the evil acts he commits.

The cross was not just ordained by God; it was specifically planned for our good because of God's love for us. Romans 5:6-8 tells us, 'You see, at just the right time, when we were still powerless, Christ died for the ungodly.

---

6 Psalm 118:1

7 Exodus 34:6

8 Acts 2:23

Very rarely will anyone die for a righteous man, though for a good man someone might possibly dare to die. But God demonstrates his own love for us in this: While we were still sinners, Christ died for us.' In His great love for us, God saved us in the only way that would allow Him to be both just and merciful. Christ's blood ransomed our souls by satisfying God's righteous wrath. Sometimes, in this day and age, we are not comfortable speaking about the wrath and judgment of God. However, if we fail to understand the wrath and destruction that we had fully earned by our sin, we will never comprehend the loving mercy poured out for us at the cross. In a sense, the cross acts as a sponge and soaks up the wrath of God on our behalf. The death we deserved was fully put on Him, so that we might receive reconciliation and relationship with God the Father. God's holiness is fully satisfied at the cross and His love is fully exemplified to His people. Jesus foreshadowed this love when speaking to His disciples by saying, 'Greater love has no one than this, that he lay down his life for his friends.'[9]

If we ever doubt God's goodness or His sovereignty, we must always go back to the cross. His goodness ordained that your sentence of death would be commuted because another stepped into your place and accepted the punishment on your behalf. In the greatest love imaginable, He has brought you to Himself. As you meditate on the cross, I hope you will let the reality of the gift given to you settle deep into your heart. Think of Paul's statement: 'He who did not spare his own Son, but gave him up for us all – how will he not also, along with him, graciously give us all things?'[10]

In light of the cross, can you imagine how offensive our coveting and discontentment must be to God? Christ faced the reality and humility of the cross and ransomed our souls from death. God demonstrated in the most sacrificial way

---

9 John 15:13

10 Romans 8:32

possible that He works all things for our good; yet we still fail to trust His provision. How can we go about grumbling and complaining about the size of our houses or the type of car we are driving when Christ gave His blood for our sakes? Can any earthly longing compare to what is ours in Christ? Place any earthly jewel beside the treasure found in Christ and it will appear as but dust. Our coveting exposes that we have set our hearts upon earthly gain. The more we seek our treasure outside of Christ, the more we falsely believe that God is lacking in His goodness to us. Essentially, our coveting accuses God of a failure to reign well over the events in our lives.

Failing to rightly reflect, remember and rejoice that God has given His own Son on our behalf leads to ingratitude and discontentment. In contrast, when we daily set our minds on God's goodness to us in Christ, our lives take on a new attitude and direction. While the cry of the covetous is 'Life's not fair', the cry of the contented Christian is 'Life's not fair … in my favor.' The contented Christian woman realizes fully that Christ unfairly faced suffering and death in order that she might live. Life has been unfair, but in *her* favor! The death and judgment she earned by her works have been placed on Christ. This redemption fills her with gratitude and thanksgiving that overflows into every area of her life. In mercy, every Christian has been given the perfect righteousness of Jesus, based on nothing we have done. Since He has given us the most costly item He had to give, we must bear with patience and trust Him when He withholds items. Even our sufferings and struggles must be viewed in the light of the cross. No matter what hardships He brings into your life, He has given you the one thing that can never be taken: the salvation of your soul from death.

It was this thought that allowed Horatio Spafford to deal with the horrific death of his four daughters. In 1873, his wife Anna and their four daughters boarded an ocean liner to sail to Europe. Horatio was delayed due to business and decided to follow afterwards. The ship carrying his family was rammed by a British vessel and sank within minutes. Anna was found alive, but all four daughters drowned. Anna telegrammed him, 'Saved alone. What shall I do…?' He immediately came to join her in Europe, and on the journey the captain showed him the spot where his four daughters had perished. He recorded the one assurance that brought him comfort in the hymn 'It is Well with My Soul.' The second stanza reads, 'Though Satan should buffet, though trials should come, Let this blest assurance control: That Christ has regarded my helpless estate and hath shed His own blood for my soul.' The reality of God's loving-kindness at the cross does not spare us from the hardships of life in a fallen world. We will each experience difficulties and struggles here that may not be eased on this side of eternity. Certainly the Spaffords' grief and sorrow continued until they joined their children in heaven. However, in the midst of this great struggle, Spafford possessed an inner contentment that allowed him to say on the most difficult day, 'It is well with my soul.' His reconciliation with the Father brought solace and comfort that could withstand even the most painful of trials.

In a similar way, it is through remembering and reflecting upon God's goodness and sovereignty that we can find contentment when facing unplanned or unwanted circumstances. Our belief that all our days are ordained by His loving and providential plan is a powerful weapon in our battle with discontentment and coveting. The fact that we are chosen by God and brought into His family fills our life with meaning and purpose. Nothing that happens in our lives comes by random chance, but instead, all is sifted through the Father's loving plan for our life. He never forgets us, and He withholds things only in love. Every season of struggle, longing and waiting is full of meaning and purpose in His plan for our lives. None of these moments are wasted in God's economy. It is so easy to get caught up in the comparison trap and spend our lives contemplating how to acquire more. As we do this, we begin to equate God's goodness with how often He gives us what we want. This wrong understanding will lead us to a life of craving in which we are never satisfied. In contrast, a life of joy and peace is found in believing that God will give us all we need for life and godliness. As we grow to trust that He is working all things for our good, we will begin to desire what He provides with a peaceful acceptance, as well as a joyful anticipation. However, this requires us to gain an understanding of what our true purpose is and what exactly it means for God to be working all things for our good.

The Great Rebellion: Unbelief in Our Purpose

Our second problem that causes us to covet is unbelief regarding our purpose in this life. If we have a temporal view of life, then we will naturally covet all that this world has to offer. The quest for the perfect life here is rooted in the false belief that this world is all that awaits us. Instead, the Bible sets forth a very different view of our purpose and God's plan for our greatest good.

Created for relationship with God

From Genesis to Revelation, the Bible speaks of God's desire for and pursuit of a relationship with His people. The original and perfect relationship between God and man that existed in the Garden of Eden was marred by the sin of Adam. All of human history from that point on is God's pursuit of His people and their rebellion from Him because of the sin passed down from Adam. Broken by sin, we could not choose God, nor could He be in relationship with us, because our sin separated us from His holiness.

In spite of the sinfulness of man, God spoke to His people Israel through the prophets, declaring time and time again His desire for a people set apart to be His own. In Jeremiah, God speaks of a new covenant that He will make, declaring,

> 'I will put my law in their minds and write it on their hearts. I will be their God and they will be my people. No longer will a man teach his neighbor, or a man his brother, saying, "Know the LORD," because they will all know me, from the least of them to the greatest,' declares the LORD. 'For I will forgive their wickedness and will remember their sins no more.'[11]

God spoke of the forgiveness and grace that would come at the cross that would allow us adoption as children of God. It is not simply that our past sins are forgiven; He also imputes all of Christ's righteousness to us. In Christ's righteousness, we can come into relationship with the Father and experience abundant life. Our greatest good in this life is not to attain a house, a husband, children or a wonderful job. Our lives find fulfillment and meaning when we come into relationship with the Father.

The prophet Isaiah also called the people of Israel to find their satisfaction in a relationship with the Father. He calls out,

> 'Come, all you who are thirsty, come to the waters; and you who have no money, come, buy and eat! Come, buy wine and milk without money and without cost. Why spend money on what is not bread, and your labor on what does not satisfy? Listen, listen to me, and eat what is good, and your soul will delight in the richest of fare. Give ear and come to me; hear me, that your soul may live.'[12]

Isaiah calls the people out of a life spent on temporal pleasures that will not satisfy, into a relationship with the Father. He calls them to come, so that their soul may live and delight in the richest of fare. In a similar manner, David exhorts, 'Taste and see that the LORD is good; blessed is the man who takes refuge in him.'[13] Asaph rightly questions, 'Whom have I in heaven but you? And earth has nothing I desire besides you. My flesh and my heart may fail, but

11 Jeremiah 31:31-34

12 Isaiah 55:1-3

13 Psalm 34:8

God is the strength of my heart and my portion forever.'[14] Each of these men speaks of a satisfaction he experienced as he entered into relationship with the Father. No other fount can satisfy the thirst that is quenched as we come to know our Creator. It is our relationship with the Lord that fills our life and brings contentment. Our coveting is a sign that we are attempting to find refreshment in worldly gains that will never satisfy. Essentially, coveting reveals our disbelief that God is enough to satisfy us. We rebel from a relationship with him in our pursuit of gaining life here. This unbelief can lead to years of searching for significance in material possessions, earthly relationships, and worldly enjoyments that will never truly bring the fulfillment we long to possess. Believing that our relationship with the Father is our true purpose frees us from these vain pursuits. He is faithful to cultivate our relationship with Him through all the means and circumstances He brings into our lives.

The Westminster Shorter Catechism explains our purpose in a similar way by stating, 'Man's chief end is to glorify God, and to enjoy him forever.' We were created to enjoy the Father by being in relationship with Him. As we know Him and grow in our affection for Him, we will glorify Him. John Piper explains the symbiotic nature of these two purposes in this way, 'God's quest to be glorified and our quest to be satisfied reach their goal in this one experience: our delight in God which overflows in praise.'[15] Thus, enjoying God leads us to our chief end: glorifying Him in all things.

CHOSEN TO GLORIFY GOD

Our purpose is to know and enjoy God, which leads us to glorify Him. When you come into the family of God, you become part of a people belonging to God, 'that you may declare the praises of him who called you out of darkness into

14 Psalm 73:25-26

15 John Piper, *Desiring God* (Sisters, OR: Multnomah Press, 1986), p. 53.

his wonderful light.'[16] We glorify God most as we worship and enjoy Him. We also glorify Him as our lives become increasingly transformed into the image of Christ. Ephesians tells us that He chose us 'to be holy and blameless in his sight.'[17] Peter tells us that we were chosen 'for obedience to Jesus Christ and sprinkling by his blood.' We are not simply chosen to spend eternity with God in heaven; we are chosen for transformation into His image here on earth.

I hope you hear in these verses the important role you have in human history. The God of the entire universe set you apart, before the creation of the world, to be adopted as His child through Christ. You are a chosen person, part of a royal priesthood and holy nation, a person belonging to God.[18] In every experience you go through, God is at work in your life. While it may seem like you are stuck, waiting and forgotten, God's Word says that you are part of the greatest story ever told. At every turn, God is working for your good.

Our problem is that we think we know what is good for us. We convince ourselves that God's goodness to us will come in the form of our choosing – healing, rest, better friendships, a spouse, a child, or a better job. However, our ideas about what is good are not always the same as God's ideas. In order to understand the good that God wants for us, we must look at the larger context of Romans 8:28. The verse begins, 'And we know that in all things God works for the good of those who love him, who have been called according to his purpose.' The passage continues, 'For those God foreknew he also predestined to be conformed to the likeness of his Son, that he might be the firstborn among many brothers.' At every moment, God is working to conform each of us into the likeness of Christ. Thus,

16 1 Peter 2:9

17 Ephesians 1:4

18 1 Peter 2:9

whatever we lack, it is so we will grow to look more like Christ. Whatever we are given, it is so we will grow to look more like Christ. Both our blessings and our trials propel us towards this ultimate and better good. C.S. Lewis describes this process in the following way:

> 'Imagine yourself as a living house. God comes in to rebuild that house. At first, perhaps, you can understand what He is doing. He is getting the drains right and stopping the leaks in the roof and so on: you knew that those jobs needed doing and so you are not surprised. But presently He starts knocking the house about in a way that hurts abominably and does not seem to make sense. What on earth is He up to? The explanation is that He is building quite a different house from the one you thought of – throwing out a new wing here, putting on an extra floor there, running up towers, making courtyards. You thought you were going to be made into a decent little cottage: but He is building a palace. He intends to come and live in it Himself.'[19]

God does not promise that our life here on earth will be one of ease or comfort. He does promise to transform our lowly bodies so they will be like His glorious body. If we want to fight our inordinate desires, we must realize and believe that our desires are so much less than what God desires for us. We also must realize that our desires and longings show that we are actually made for something much more.

GRANTED A NEW CITIZENSHIP

Lastly, coveting reveals our unbelief about our citizenship. Our persistent desire to gain life here and to acquire all that this world has to offer reveals our belief that this life is the destination, rather than a journey to our final home. The scriptures describe us as strangers and aliens, with our citizenship in heaven. That truth should dramatically change how we view and live life here.

---

19 C.S. Lewis, *Mere Christianity* (New York: Macmillan Pub. Co., 1984), p. 174

I experienced the feeling of being a citizen of one land, yet residing in another, when we lived overseas in Scotland. The fact that we knew we would only be there a few years caused us to live quite differently. We moved there with only four suitcases. We rented a furnished flat rather than buying new furniture. I shopped less because I knew that most items I bought there would remain there when we moved. Basically, we traveled lightly in our time there and experienced great freedom from the responsibility that comes from ownership. We also experienced the feeling of being different from others around us. I used words like 'faucet' and 'garbage can' instead of 'tap' and 'rubbish bin.' My daughter wore diapers, while all her friends wore 'nappies'. At times, we longed for the comforts of home and the dear friends who seemed so far away. However, we also fully lived there and engaged in that world. We made new friends, worked jobs and had our first child. Knowing that we were not home changed how we lived, but it did not stop us from living.

Each of us should have a similar expectation as we reside here on earth, knowing that our citizenship is in heaven. If we want to fight coveting, we will have to take our eyes off this present world and catch a vision of our heavenly home. We must view this earthly experience as a journey, not the destination itself. When we are traveling far away from home, we should expect that we will occasionally feel lonely. We should expect that everything will not always go as planned. We should expect that dearly loved ones will sometimes be out of our reach. It is all part of the journey. Yet, we can still make deep friendships, enjoy wonderful moments and experience abundant life along the way. We live, even as we journey. Yet, we change our expectations of how we plan to live because we know all the comforts of home await us in heaven. The book of Revelation speaks to this glorious hope when John hears a voice saying, 'Behold, the tabernacle of God is with men, and he will dwell with them, and they shall be his people, and God himself shall be with them, and be their God. And God shall wipe away all tears from their eyes; and there shall be no more death, neither sorrow, nor crying, neither shall there be any more pain: for the former things are passed away.' We will finally be home when we dwell with God. All will be right and all our longings will be fully satisfied with the Lord Himself. We must grow in our belief that our heavenly home awaits, in order to experience abundant life in the present.

THE GREAT FAILURE: UNBELIEF IN OUR RELATIONSHIPS

Thus far, we have discussed that coveting is unbelief in the character of God, as well as rebellion against God's true purpose for our lives here on earth. Lastly, I want us to briefly touch upon one other reason that we covet. Often, coveting results because of unbelief in how we are to relate to our neighbor. Our covetous responses show that we view our neighbor as a measuring stick of God's love. If they have something that we do not, then God is failing to be good to us. If we have something our neighbor does not, then we feel blessed and special. Determining God's love for us (or lack of love) based on our neighbor's life divides us from those around us. It also presupposes that fairness is the best way God can bless His children.

Instead, God knows that each of His children are individually formed and made. He created each of us in a particular way and brings to our lives just what we need in order to be conformed into His image. One person may be equipped well to live with riches and not fall into temptation. Another person may be better off with less income because the Lord knows riches will be a snare for her soul. One person may get married just out of college and the Lord use her marriage to sanctify and change her. Another woman may remain single and the Lord uses that experience to sanctify and change her.

In order to illustrate this point, imagine a potter making a set of china for his cabinet. He is making two pieces, a teacup and a plate. The teacup thinks to herself, 'I wish I was a plate. The plate has so many more uses than I do. The plate gets to come out of the cabinet every day and is much more practical than I am. Its flat surface can be used to hold so many wonderful foods. I am only good for holding tea. Why did He create me this way?' The plate, on the other hand, looks over at the teacup and thinks, 'How great would it be if I were a tea cup? The potter took so much time to create the gentle curves of the teacup and He only uses her on special occasions. I am so ordinary. I am more chipped and worn. I also had to go through a much hotter fire in the kiln because I am not as delicate. I wish that I could have the life of a tea cup.' Can you imagine such a strange conversation? Both items are created for the potter's purposes. They each, in different ways, are useful to the potter and display the potter's glory. The potter knows exactly what type of clay was needed, how hot to heat the kiln and what purpose they serve in his china cabinet. Their comparison just leads to discontentment with the potter, as well as discontentment with their own design.

In the same way, our Lord knows your frame intimately. He knit you together in your mother's womb. He ordained all of your days before one of them came to be. He knows your frame and understands how to care for you and shape you more than you even know yourself. Of course, the Lord does not use the same tools on each of His children. He knows exactly what struggles and blessings each person needs to make that person more like Christ. His plan is not to make your life just like everyone else's, but to make each individual shine forth His glory as He uses our differences to display the beauty of the body of Christ. Our comparison game keeps us from enjoying other people and robs us of enjoying the work that Christ is doing in our own life.

In contrast, the Scriptures call us to love our neighbor as ourselves. We are to look for their good and rejoice in the blessings in their lives. When they suffer, we are to suffer by their side. If they are not Christians, we speak the gospel to them, hoping they will come to Christ. If they are Christians, we build them up in the faith, knowing that by doing so, we are building up our own body. We are not in competition with those around us. We are on the journey with them.

As we close this chapter, I hope you realize that our covetous desires do not result from deprivation on a physical level. Our covetous desires are a consequence of spiritual deprivation: unbelief. Coveting does not result because we don't *have* something. We covet because we fail to believe something. Unbelief in God, our purpose and our neighbor leads us to inordinate desires. Coveting causes us to break what Jesus referred to as the greatest commandment: to 'love the Lord your God with all your heart and with all your soul and with all your mind.'[20] When we covet, we turn our affections away from God and towards the object of our desire. Coveting also causes us to break the second greatest commandment: to 'Love your neighbor as yourself.'[21] When we covet, we view our neighbor as a measuring stick of God's love for us. In order to fight this battle and weed out this sin, we must replace our unbelief with proper belief concerning God's character, God's purpose for us, and the true worth of our neighbor. This is not a matter of purely intellectual assertion of right belief, but is part of the ongoing process of getting to know God and learning from His Word. In the next chapter, we will start unpacking the pattern coveting takes as we look at the examples of two coveters: Eve in the Garden of Eden and Achan in the Land of Canaan.

---

20 Matthew 22:37

21 Matthew 22:39

Questions for Personal Reflection and Group Discussion

1. How does what we believe about someone affect our ability to trust them? How does belief affect our desires?
2. How is covetousness similar to idolatry? How is it different?
3. In what ways does covetousness betray a lack of belief in God? As you consider your life, are you confident that you have come to faith in Christ alone?
4. Read Psalm 139:1-16. What are the various ways David states that God is reigning over the events in his life?
5. How do we see both God's reign over sinful acts and man's responsibility for his own sin in Genesis 50:19-20? How do we see this truth in Acts 2:23?
6. How does our belief that God is both good and sovereign affect our ability to wait with patience when our present longings are not fulfilled?
7. Read Romans 8:28-30. What promises do you see in these verses? What is not promised? From these verses, what would you say is God's greatest hope for your life? What is His plan for you, regardless of your circumstances?
8. How does the understanding that God is working all things for your good change how you view the hardships, struggles and unmet desires you are currently facing?
9. Read Romans 8:31-32. How does remembering and reflecting upon Christ's sacrificial love at the cross help us to trust Him and wait with patience for our longings? Why would our coveting be so offensive to God in light of the cross?
10. The Westminster Shorter Catechism states, 'Man's chief end is to glorify God, and to enjoy him forever.' How does this compare to the chief end of the covetous? What

would you say is the 'chief end' of most people? How would it change your life to start living with this purpose?

11. Read 1 Peter 2:11. How does he describe the Christian? What does he encourage them to do? What would it look like to live as a stranger or alien?

12. Read Philippians 3:18-21. How does believing that our citizenship is in heaven help us to combat our covetous desires?

13. C. S. Lewis states the following, 'Aim at heaven and you will get earth thrown in. Aim at earth and you get neither.' How have you seen this principle work out in your own life? What does it look like to fully engage and live in this present world, while putting your hope in the next?

14. Read Matthew 22:36-40. How do our covetous desires lead us to break both the command to love God and the command to love our neighbor?

15. Read the following quote from David Macintyre:

    > Much, very much, has often to be accomplished in us before we are fitted to employ worthily the gifts we covet. And God effects this preparation of heart largely by delaying to grant our request at once, and so holding us in the truth of His presence until we are brought into a spiritual understanding of the will of Christ for us in this respect.[22]

    Can you think of a situation where God's timing afforded you necessary growth so that you would be able to better use (or enjoy) the item you longed for? How does waiting at times ready us for the gifts that God gives us?

16. The best way to combat our wrong desires is to grow our right desires for God. What are the means that help you to love God in deeper ways? How can you live a life of greater worship and thankfulness?

---

22 David Macintyre, *The Hidden Life of Prayer* (Fearn, Scotland: Christian Focus, 1993) p. 101.

3 The Pattern of Coveting

He takes Eve when she is near the tree. When the tree is in view the force of the temptation doubles. It is much easier to tempt when he has the presence of an object to excite the lust that lies dormant in the heart. If the Christian lets the object of temptation draw near, Satan anticipates that his scheme will soon be effective. Therefore, if it is our desire not to yield to sin, we must not walk by or sit at the door of the occasion. Do not look with a wandering eye at the beauty by which you would be taken captive. Do not parley in your thoughts with that which you do not wish to also take into your heart.

WILLIAM GURNALL

Voices From the Past, p. 175

3

The Pattern of Coveting:

See, Covet, Take and Hide

Thus far, we have unpacked the definition of coveting and considered the primary reason our desires spiral out of control. In short, we have covered *what* coveting is and *why* we fall into this sin. In this chapter, we will begin to examine *how* coveting progresses in our lives. We will study the pattern that coveting takes and how it develops from an inward sin to outward harm of others. In order to accomplish this, we will examine two Biblical characters: Eve and Achan. As we probe into their lives, we will notice that their stories follow a similar pattern of covetous desires and painful consequences. We will close the chapter by observing how this same pattern often works in our hearts, with similar effect.

The Envy of Eve

A good place to begin a thorough study of coveting is at the first instance of this sin recorded in the Bible. Unfortunately for us all, the earliest example of coveting happens almost as soon as the Biblical narrative begins. In the third chapter of the book of Genesis, we read of the story of Adam and Eve and the fall of man. Before considering their struggle with sin, we will review the setting in which Adam and Eve lived.

The paradise of the Garden

Genesis chapter one gives us a play-by-play account of the creation of the world. We are told, 'In the beginning, God created the heavens and the earth.'[1] God initiates. God acts. He begins earth's history by simply speaking it into existence. Each day God creates, filling the earth with water, land, plants and animals and declares all of it to be good. The culmination of His creation occurs on the sixth day as God forms man and woman into His own image.

After God creates Adam and Eve, He does not simply leave them on their own; He gives them instructions about how to live. He commands them to be fruitful and multiply, to have dominion over the animals and to eat the plants for food. In Genesis 2, God demonstrates His care for Adam and Eve as He plants a garden in Eden and places them there to work and keep it. He puts two special trees in the Garden – the tree of life and the tree of the knowledge of good and evil. Adam is free to eat from every tree in the Garden except the tree of the knowledge of good and evil. God instructs Adam not to eat of it, promising that if he eats of it he will certainly die. God provides Adam and Eve everything they need: companionship, purpose, dominion, and a bountiful sustenance. Everything around them was good, and God was pleased with all that He created.

This peaceful tranquility did not last long. Satan, cloaked in the form of a serpent, comes to tempt Eve. He begins his attack by maligning the Word of God, asking, 'Did God actually say, "You shall not eat of any tree in the garden"?'[2] In return, Eve corrects the serpent and tells him that in truth, they are allowed to eat from every tree in the Garden,

---

1 Genesis 1:1

2 Genesis 3:1

except one. Eve's response indicates that Adam had fully instructed Eve of God's commands, that she was aware of which tree to avoid, and that the consequence of eating from it would be death. Satan, realizing that Eve knew what God had commanded, begins a new attack by questioning God's character in two areas: His sovereignty and His goodness.

Satan's attack on God's sovereignty comes when he denies the absolute nature of God's Word. The serpent says to Eve, 'You will not surely die.'[3] With this statement, he leads Eve to doubt the certainty of what God has said. He calls into question God's authority, power and integrity. Is God true to His Word? Is He able to do all that He has said He will do? These doubts of His sovereignty are quickly built upon as the serpent questions God's goodness. He continues, 'For God knows that when you eat of it your eyes will be opened, and you will be like God, knowing good and evil.' Implicit in this statement is the notion that God is keeping something good from Adam and Eve. It also suggests that God is keeping something from them because He wants it only for Himself. John Calvin comments, '[The serpent] censures God as being moved by jealousy: and as having given the command concerning the tree, for the purpose of keeping man in an inferior rank.'[4] The serpent tempts Eve to doubt God's Word and His goodness to her. He stirs up discontentment in her heart, as well as a longing to rule, rather than be ruled. Do not miss the fact that Eve, even in the middle of all the goodness of Eden, finds herself longing for the one thing forbidden. In the midst of perfect circumstances, unbelief can still arise. We choose what to allow our thoughts to linger upon and consider. As Eve ponders these false ideas, the pattern of coveting begins.

---

3 Genesis 3:4

4 John Calvin, *Calvin's Commentaries* Volume 1 (Grand Rapids: Baker Book House Company, 1993) p. 150.

The Pattern of Coveting

Prompted by unbelief, the pattern that coveting takes is simply this: see, covet, take, and hide. A person sees something he does not have, sinfully desires that item, takes it, and then, once the item is acquired, attempts to hide what he has done. As Genesis continues, Eve finds herself ensnared in this pattern. After hearing the serpent's attack on God's character, Genesis 3:6 states:

> So when the woman *saw* that the tree was good for food, and that it was a delight to the eyes, and that the tree was to be *desired* to make one wise, she *took* of its fruit and ate, and she also gave some to her husband who was with her and he ate. Then the eyes of both were opened and they knew they were naked. And they sewed fig leaves together and made themselves loincloths. And they heard the sound of the Lord God walking in the garden in the cool of the day, and the man and his wife *hid* themselves from the presence of the Lord God among the trees of the garden.' [emphasis added][5]

Eve saw

The pattern began for Eve as she saw the fruit. Surely, she had looked upon the fruit of this tree before, but this gaze of Eve was different because of the state of her heart. Calvin comments, 'She could previously behold the tree with such sincerity, that no desire to eat of it affected her mind; for the faith she had in the Word of God was the best guardian of her heart, and of all her senses. But now, after the heart had declined from faith, and from obedience to the Word, she corrupted both herself and all her senses, and depravity was diffused through all parts of her soul as well as her body.'[6] The fruit had not changed, but Eve's eyes saw the fruit in a new light because of her unbelief. It was good to

5 Genesis 3:6-8, ESV.

6 John Calvin, *Calvin's Commentaries*, Volume 1, p. 151.

eat, beautiful to look upon and could give wisdom. Her focus narrowed and shifted from seeing the pleasures of the Garden around her, to concentrating on the one item forbidden.

Eve coveted

As we discussed in chapter one, we can know that our longing has turned to coveting when we long for an object that is clearly outside of God's revealed will for us. The fruit from this tree was forbidden, but the text tells us that Eve desired it for gaining wisdom. The root word for desirable in this instance is the same word used for covet – *chamad*. In a sense, Eve saw that the fruit was covetable, or worthy to be coveted. She chose to think upon it, consider it and desire it, even though God instructed her to avoid this fruit and gave her a bounty to enjoy. Satan wants us to believe that we cannot control what we long after or that if we have a longing, it must be good, in spite of God's instruction. It is one of his most damaging lies, keeping us enslaved to years of worthless pursuits. Although we cannot always choose what we see, we can choose what we set our heart upon. Certainly, Eve could have desired the fruit of the tree of life, also situated in the Garden. The choice was before her: life or death. Eve set her heart upon the forbidden fruit, wanting its wisdom, and chose to assert her independence.

Eve took

Eve's covetous heart led to outward action. Here we can clearly observe the begetting nature of the sin. She took the fruit and ate, and she also gave some to her husband. While this is the first instance of outward rebellion, the rebellion of unbelief could actually be considered the first sin that occurred in the Garden. From Eve's unbelief flowed coveting, and from the sin of coveting flowed her disobedience of eating the forbidden fruit. In her own sin, she led her husband astray. The tempted now became the temptress. She who was given to man as a companion and helper to share in all the pleasures of Eden becomes, instead, a helper in his destruction.

Eve hid

With the fruit came the wisdom Eve desired, although not in the form she wanted. Both she and Adam now realize, to their shame, they are naked. In order to hide their nakedness, they make clothes out of fig leaves, trying to cover themselves. When they hear the sound of the Lord, Adam and Eve attempt to hide themselves among the trees in the Garden. It is to no avail. The Lord, who made them and knows them, surely knew of their disobedience. Even so, they attempt to hide from their omniscient Creator. In our fallen state, we attempt to hide what we have done from everyone, including ourselves.

Consequences

At this point in the narrative, God pronounces various judgments and consequences for the serpent, Eve and Adam. From one sin flows much pain. Eve selfishly considered only herself as she coveted. She did not consider the results of her choices. Her sin had adverse effects on herself, her family, her community and her Lord. Eve's physical body was cursed as her pains in childbearing were multiplied. Her emotional state was cursed, as her desire would be for her husband, yet he would rule over her. Adam, her only family up to that point, suffered as he was led into his own sin by her example. From his sin flowed the curse on the ground and on all of his work. Adam and Eve were banished from the community of the Garden of Eden, unable to eat the fruit of the tree of life. All those who would come after Adam were marred by the sinful nature. As Paul tells us, 'just as sin entered the world through one man, and death through sin' so also 'death came to all men, because all sinned.'[7] Adam gave

---

7 Romans 5:12

to all who would come after him the taint of his sin and, with that, the taste of death. Lastly, and most importantly, God's glory was affected by Eve's covetous choices. Adam and Eve were placed in the Garden with the special distinction of being made in the image of God. They were commanded to be fruitful and multiply and by doing so would fill the earth with the image of the Creator. They glorified Him because they were made in His image. With their fall into sin, the image that once perfectly reflected God's glory was marred and broken. From such a seemingly inconsequential sin, terrible consequences flowed. It might be easy to believe that these negative consequences were so great only because of the perfection that surrounded Adam and Eve and the fact that they were our first parents. Does our coveting really lead to such troubling consequences, in both our lives and those around us? Is God's glory affected by this pattern in our lives as well? In order to begin to answer these questions, we will move out of Eden and into Canaan. We will observe another example, Achan, and how his coveting followed a similar pattern and similar set of consequences as Eve's.

Coveting in Canaan

The story of Achan takes place in the book of Joshua, after the battle of Jericho. Prior to this battle, the people of Israel had just finished wandering in the desert for forty years. During these years, they lived in tents and fed upon manna from heaven. They lived without homes, fields and crops, and could only keep the possessions they could carry with them as they wandered. Upon the death of Moses, Joshua was given the task of leading the people into the Promised Land. Miraculously, God parts the river Jordan, and the people cross to the other side and find themselves in the land of Canaan – the land promised more than four hundred years before to their father Abraham. Soon after crossing, the Lord instructs Joshua, 'See, I have delivered

Jericho into your hands.'[8] He tells Joshua to have the people march around the city for six days, and on the seventh day, they were commanded to shout. At this loud clamor, the walls came down, allowing them entrance into the city. However, they were to destroy everything in the city with the following warning, 'But you, keep yourselves from the things devoted to destruction, lest when you have devoted them you take any of the devoted things and make the camp of Israel a thing for destruction and bring trouble upon it. But all silver and gold, and every vessel of bronze and iron, are holy to the Lord; they shall go into the treasury of the Lord.'[9]

The Israelites won the battle, and at the end of this chapter we are told that the Lord was with Joshua and that his fame spread throughout the land. All seems to be progressing well in the land of Canaan until we turn to the next chapter and read, 'But the people of Israel broke faith in regard to the devoted things, for Achan the son of Carmi, son of Zabdi, son of Zerah, of the tribe of Judah, took some of the devoted things. And the anger of the Lord burned against the people of Israel.'[10]

The people of Israel have finally come into a land of their own, and already they have sinned against the Lord! However, Joshua is unaware of the breach that occurred and sends men out to attack the city of Ai. This attack goes poorly and thirty-six men lose their lives, while the rest are forced to flee the battle. The entire nation of Israel, fresh from their first taste of victory, is now full of fear, and their hearts lack courage. Joshua cries out to the Lord, wondering what has happened and why He has allowed His people to lose this battle. God instructs Joshua to bring the people of Israel before Him, tribe

---

8 Joshua 6:2

9 Joshua 6:18-19, ESV.

10 Joshua 7:1, ESV.

by tribe, until the man who has taken some of the devoted things is discovered. From the tribe of Judah, Achan is chosen and confesses, 'It is true! I have sinned against the LORD, the God of Israel. This is what I have done: When I *saw* in the plunder a beautiful robe from Babylonia, two hundred shekels of silver and a wedge of gold weighing fifty shekels, I *coveted* them and *took* them. They are *hidden* in the ground inside my tent, with the silver underneath'[emphasis added].[11] Here again, we see the same pattern taking place: see, covet, take and hide.

Achan saw

In the midst of the battle of Jericho, Achan saw a beautiful robe, silver and gold. Once again, this pattern of coveting begins with the eyes. Achan, surrounded by a battle, still took the time to look at the items he was commanded to destroy. I am certain that many of these items must have been tempting to the Israelites. They had been wandering for forty years in the desert, and here, all around them, were items they needed. There were homes, livestock, clothing, as well as silver and gold. These items would provide the stability and comforts they longed for after years of wandering. However, with eyes of faith, one can see that true security only comes from the Lord. Thus, all of the other Israelites, by faith, saw these items and obediently placed them in the fire to be burned. Achan, however, viewed these items through the lens of his unbelief. His eyes had also witnessed forty years of the provision of manna in the desert, the parting of the Jordan River, and, just that very day, the walls of Jericho miraculously falling to the ground. Achan had seen the goodness and provision of the Lord, yet he chose to let his eyes rest upon that which the Lord had forbidden. What we choose to set our gaze upon is often a reflection of the idolatry in our heart.

---

11 Joshua 7:20-21

Achan coveted

While Eve coveted wisdom, Achan coveted material possessions. Perhaps he believed that they would provide him comfort and security. Perhaps he thought they would give him status and respect. For whatever reason, he chose to set his heart upon these items and long for them inordinately. Was it wrong for Achan to want possessions of his own? No, his longing was a good one. In fact, in every battle after Jericho, all the Israelites were allowed to plunder the cities they overtook. They were given the silver, gold, clothing, livestock and homes. These were blessings the Lord wanted to give to His people. However, He first and foremost wanted their affection, trust and obedience. Matthew Henry comments on this notion after the second battle at Ai when they were allowed to take all the plunder:

> Observe, how Achan who caught at forbidden spoil lost that, and life, and all, but the rest of the people who had conscientiously refrained from the accursed thing were quickly recompensed for their obedience with the spoil of Ai. The way to have the comfort of what God allows is to forbear what he forbids us. No man shall lose by his self-denial; let God have his dues first and then all will be clean to us and sure, 1 Kings 17:13. God did not bring them to these goodly cities and houses filled with all good things, to tantalize them with the sight of that which they might not touch; but, having received the first-fruits from Jericho, the spoil of Ai, and all the cities which thenceforward came into their hands, they might take for a prey to themselves.[12]

Achan failed to trust the Lord enough to forbear what was forbidden. This lack of trust quickly led him to take.

Achan took

Achan's unbelief first took hold of his affections as he coveted and quickly turned to outward action as he took the items. In

12 Matthew Henry, *Matthew Henry's Commentary on the Whole Bible*, Volume 2 (Peabody, Massachusetts: Hendrickson Publishing, 1991) p. 35.

this instance we can clearly observe the begetting nature of coveting. His greed conceived and brought forth stealing from the Lord. The silver and gold were to be placed in the treasury of the Lord. Instead, Achan took these items for himself.

Achan hid

The irony of this story is that Achan took a beautiful robe, silver and gold, and then he was forced to hide them under his tent. He did not get to enjoy the silver and gold or wear the beautiful robe. Our forbidden spoils or unjust gains will never bring us the life we believe they will. They promise much, but deliver only painful regret and dire consequences. Achan must have felt the fear of being found out, and in a similar way to Adam and Eve, he attempted to hide what he had done. As much as we try to hide our actions from others, they are not hidden from the Lord. Nor are the consequences limited to Achan only, but they extend to his family, community and the Lord's glory.

Consequences

Achan himself paid dearly for his sin. God's judgment was upon him and he was taken outside of the camp and stoned to death. Secondly, Achan's family and all of his possessions were stoned and their remains burned in utter destruction. His hopes to provide them with the luxuries of Canaan ended in providing them suffering and death. The community of Israel also suffered greatly from Achan's sin. Thirty-six men lost their lives in the battle of Ai. This battle was lost because of Achan's sin, and it is the only time in the entire book of Joshua that we are told of any of the Israelites losing their lives. Thirty-six families lost husbands, brothers, fathers, and uncles. Also, the passage tells us that all of the Israelites lost courage and became fearful because of the defeat at Ai.[13] Lastly, and most importantly, God's great

13 Joshua 7:5

name was affected by Achan's sin. God chose to attach His name to His people, the Israelites, and when they failed, His name did not receive the glory He deserved. Joshua speaks to this notion as he laments, 'O Lord, what can I say, when Israel has turned their backs before their enemies! For the Canaanites and all the inhabitants of the land will hear of it and will surround us and cut off our name from the earth. And what will you do for your great name?'[14] God's glory is affected by the actions of His people.

The similarities in the stories of Eve and Achan point to the pattern of coveting. Both of these stories began with unbelief that led to sinful actions which bore painful consequences for many. To close this chapter, we will consider how this pattern appears in our own lives when our unbelief leads us to see, covet, take and hide.

We see

Our coveting begins first and foremost with our eyes. We look over the fence into another person's life and believe that the grass is greener. If God has withheld something from us, we begin to see it everywhere. If a woman is longing for a husband or in a troubled marriage, it seems that she cannot go anywhere without seeing happy couples holding hands and enjoying life together. A woman longing for a baby sees pregnant women everywhere she turns. One mother notices another woman's children obediently behaving, while she struggles daily with her own children's disobedience. A woman watches as her neighbor's grown children live just down the street and visit with the grandchildren often, while hers live far away and rarely visit.

At other times, our longings result from what we see. A friend shows up in a cute outfit, and suddenly, we feel plain and out of style. We open up the latest house magazine, and our own home furnishings seem drab in comparison. We

14 Joshua 7:8-9, ESV.

see a romantic comedy and perhaps we begin to think that our own husband could bring flowers more, make us laugh more and be more attentive to our needs. Achan saw the robe, the silver and the gold, and then he began to long for these possessions to be his own. In a similar way, our seeing sometimes leads us to want something that we did not even know we wanted until we saw it.

However, I want to emphasize that seeing itself is not necessarily a problem. It is *seeing mixed with unbelief* that awakens our covetous heart. Two people can see the exact same thing and have very different reactions. Problems arise when we focus on certain items and falsely believe that our life would be fulfilled if we could just have those things. Eve focused on the fruit from the tree of the knowledge of good and evil and ignored all the other trees in the Garden. She desired only the fruit that was prohibited. Similarly, we sometimes focus our eyes on what we believe will give us more joy out of life, ignoring God's blessings around us. In many cases, we cannot change what we see. But we can become aware of our reactions to what we see, and of our tendency toward the unbelief that leads to coveting.

We covet

Eve coveted wisdom, while Achan coveted physical possessions. We covet vastly different items depending upon our life stage, personality and circumstances. Some people struggle with coveting material goods. Others covet people's affection and approval. Many women covet being in control of the circumstances in their lives. We want to be in charge of when and whom we marry, our ability to bear children and the jobs we work. Some women covet social standing and preeminence, while others long to just fit in and be like everyone else. Often, the families we grew up in and the desires of our parents shape the items that we long for as adults. Regardless, each of us, during different life stages, will struggle with the temptation to believe that our life would be more satisfied or enhanced if we could just have ________ (fill in the blank). These covetous desires can arise in even the most perfect circumstances in our lives (just look at Eve) and rob us of the joy we could have experienced.

We usually covet in the areas where we compare ourselves to others the most. We compare colleges, boyfriends, weddings, children, parents, homes, jobs, trials, gifts, ministries, grandchildren, health, and numerous other items. Usually, at the heart of this comparison trap is the mistaken belief that another person is getting it all, while we are getting second best. We sit and stew over what another has in some area and our hearts harden toward that person, as well as towards God. In our unbelief, we falsely think to ourselves that God must love them more. As these covetous desires grow in our heart, eventually we will come to the point where we wrongfully take from others and from God.

We take

As our covetous desires grow, we will eventually take from others around us or from God. While Achan and Eve actually took the physical items they longed for, usually we will take in more subtle ways. Since we may not be able to obtain the object of our desire, we take by omitting the good we should do or by harming others as a byproduct of our discontentment.

Taking assumes different forms and affects different individuals. As we spend money on our own pleasures and fail to tithe, we take from the Lord. We take away from a friend's reputation by gossiping about her or sharing confidential information. We take away from missionaries or those in need in our own community by spending carelessly, while they have great needs. We take from another's joy by failing to rejoice with her because we believe that God has failed to be good to us in some area. Our sourness about our own situation takes from her joy. We take community away from a lonely person because we fail to invite them for dinner. We take joy and peace away by busying ourselves to the point of sinful stress and worry. We take from others by failing to spend time alone with the Lord so that we can spend time on our own pleasures. Our failure to know the Lord and find life in Him affects our witness and the wisdom we have to offer those around us. We take care from others by always considering our own needs and failing to consider their needs. We take sympathy from another by failing to mourn what is difficult for them because we have compared it to our own life and have deemed their suffering 'lesser' than our own. We take glory from God by boasting of our own accomplishments instead of giving Him the praise for what He has done. We take in a variety of ways. Once we realize we have taken, in our shame, we attempt to hide what we have done.

We hide

When our seeing has led to coveting and coveting has led to taking, we often find ourselves in hiding. We hide either because we are ashamed of what we have done or because we still want to hold on to whatever we have taken unlawfully. Notice the irony for both Eve and Achan. For each, what they believed would bring them pleasure only brought ruin and misery. Eve believed that she would become like God, and instead she became a broken image bearer, attempting to hide her nakedness with fig leaves. Achan believed he would enjoy the silver, gold and the robe. However, rather than enjoying these items, he was forced to hide them in his tent and pay the ultimate penalty for his crime.

So it is with what we take unlawfully. The adulterous affair must be hidden. We hide our anger, discontentment and lack of joy by attempting to explain the difficulty of our circumstances. Our gossip is hidden under the guise of prayer requests and openness. We blame our failure to give generously on our limited resources. Rather than drawing near to God and confessing our sin, we choose to stay hidden and unable to enjoy the gifts God has given us. Our hiding separates us from relationship with others as well as closeness to God.

We suffer consequences

Just as we often follow the same sinful pattern as Eve and Achan, we also suffer multiple repercussions as they did. Their sin led to negative consequences in four primary areas: their own comfort, their family, their community and the Lord. Eve and Achan both eventually suffered death because of their choices. They also suffered the loss of future blessing. Eve was not allowed to enjoy the blessing of eating from the tree of life. Achan was not allowed to enjoy the fruits of victory in all of the other cities that the Israelites defeated. When we forcibly take what we covet, we also will suffer death and loss of future blessings. The death we experience will not always be physical in nature, but may involve the death of a dream, loss of hope or lessened enjoyment of a current blessing.

In today's society, it is unpopular to talk about the consequences of our sinful choices. We prefer to hear of the goodness, mercy and forgiveness of Christ. While it is true that God forgives the repentant whatever sins he has committed, it is also true that our actions yield consequences. God, in His faithfulness to us, exposes the painful results of unbelief. He woos us away from sinful choices by letting us taste the painful consequences in order to protect us from future unbelief. Christians suffer from addictions, STDs, jail sentences, divorces, broken relationships, bankruptcy, and health problems, often due to choices that began with coveting. All of our suffering is not the result of our covetous patterns. We suffer at times because we live in a fallen world or from the sinful choices of another. However, we must accept that at times we suffer as a consequence of our own sinful patterns.

We also must accept that our choices will have a great impact on our family. Achan's entire family shared in his destruction. A mother who covets social standing, possessions or body image will often influence her children to chase after similarly vain pursuits. Just as children who are physically abused often become abusive parents themselves, so we pass on our covetous tendencies to our children. Our impatience, discontentment, anger and worry will often become evident patterns in their lives as well. Our children love us; so, naturally, they will grow to love what we love.

Our coveting will also affect our community. The book of Joshua states that the entire community of Israel 'broke faith in regard to the devoted things, for Achan...took some of the devoted things.'[15] Achan's sin was not just treated as his own, but caused the entire camp of Israel to be defiled. Similarly, Paul likens the church community to a body. If one part suffers, then every part suffers with it.[16] This includes the trials that come upon us, as well as the sufferings that come from our sin. Consider a man who chooses to engage in marital infidelity on just one occasion. This one moment of weakness brings suffering not only to his own body and his family, but also to his community. Pastors and elders will be called in to give their personal time to care for this man and his family. They will take hours away from their own families in order to help in the healing process for this family. The hours this family spends in counseling and healing will not just affect the people counseling them, but also the people that they themselves could have ministered to in those months. Other members in the church might be more easily tempted into sin themselves or wrongly view their own sin as less significant when they learn of his infidelity. Nonbelievers consider his situation as proof that the church is no different than the world. Our covetous desires

15 Joshua 7:1, ESV.

16 1 Corinthians 12:26

bring painful consequences and affect our ability to minister to others well. As we suffer the effects of our idolatry, we cause our community to suffer with us.

Lastly, and most importantly, our covetous desires will affect God's glory. The way we live our lives says a lot about the God we worship. Our incessant cravings suggest to others that we worship a God who is not able to satisfy. A bitter spirit says that our God is not able to provide. If we claim God as our parent, yet complain about His decrees and ways, we portray God as a tyrant instead of a loving and compassionate Father. Our desire to obtain life here communicates our belief that heaven is only a possibility instead of an unseen reality. Chasing after our covetous desires shows the watching world that we believe life is found in temporal pleasures rather than the Lord Himself. Lives that should abound with joy and thanksgiving to God are often stifled by the cares of this world. Just as Eve's unbelief about God was passed on to her husband, so our unbelief will be passed on to others in our lives. God is glorified by our belief – it is the means of our salvation. It is also how we bring Him glory and honor.

As you read of these consequences, I hope you begin to feel the seriousness of this sin pattern. In fact, I hope you begin to hate it. If we are to fight this sin with vigilance, we must grow to understand it for the evil it is and the suffering it brings to many. That which falsely promises life, is, in reality, a thief that keeps on taking. We must grow in our distaste and dissatisfaction for our sin if we want to taste and see that the Lord is good. If you observe in your own actions this pattern of seeing, coveting, taking and hiding, do not despair. Christ's blood is effectual to cleanse us from the penalty of past sin, as well as the power of it in our lives today. We will spend the next chapter discussing how to put off this old pattern of unbelief and put on a new pattern of belief in order to fight our covetous desires. We will not stop longing; we will just learn to crave a much better feast.

Questions for Personal Reflection and Group Discussion

Read Genesis 3

1. In this passage, how do you observe the serpent prompting Eve towards unbelief?
2. What particular aspects of God's character do you see him attack?
3. Re-read Genesis 3:6-7. How do you see the pattern of 'see, covet, take and hide' in this passage?
4. What are the consequences that result for Adam, Eve and the serpent?
5. How do we see both God's judgment and His mercy in this passage?
6. Read Joshua 7.
7. How do you see the pattern of 'see, covet, take and hide' in this passage?
8. What are the various consequences that result from Achan's sin?
9. Why do you think Achan took the beautiful robe, the silver and the gold from the plunder? What did he believe about those possessions? What did he believe (or not believe) about God?
10. What similarities do you see between the stories of Eve and Achan? What differences?
11. Coveting usually takes the pattern of 'See, covet, take and hide.' How do you see this pattern in our world? The church? Your own heart?
12. How have you seen negative consequences result from your own coveting or the coveting of another person?

13. How does coveting tear apart our friendships and community? Have you ever been hurt by another's envy of you? Or, has your envy ever led to brokenness in a relationship with a friend?
14. Read 1 Corinthians 10:6-13. What warnings can we take from the examples of Eve and Achan? What hope can we take from Paul's words to the Corinthians?

4 The Power over Coveting

Faith may conclude that the Spirit will bring forth this fruit in me. What God has done for his people formerly are, in effect, promises too. Faith may conclude that the Lord will work in like manner in the future. If he delivered others who trusted in him, he will deliver me if I trust in him now. He is the same yesterday and forever. David conquered Goliath in the name of the Lord, and prevailed. If I go in like manner against my lusts, I shall prevail.

David Clarkson

Voices From the Past, p. 174.

4

The Power over Coveting:

The Cross of Christ

My son, John, has always been a rather picky eater. I tried in every way to set him off on a good course in the area of eating habits. I made all of his baby food in an attempt to give him fresh vegetables and the taste of real food. I began with items like peas and carrots so that he would develop a desire for savory foods before introducing sweet foods such as applesauce and pears. However, to my dismay, he quickly rejected my homemade broccoli and pea purees. Sometimes he rejected them simply on the basis of their color or texture. It was as if he knew that something else out there was more enticing, and he was just waiting for it to come along.

On his first birthday, we were celebrating with my family, and Aunt Dottie bought him a cupcake that was piled high with blue icing. I thought he might reject it because it had such a bright blue color and was a different texture than anything he had seen before. Instead of rejecting the cupcake, or even tentatively trying it, John immediately plopped his entire face into the cupcake and began sucking the icing off the top! He had found his heart's desire at last.

He did not need to learn how to love a cupcake; it came quite naturally to him. However, he cannot live on cupcakes, so over the years he has had to learn to eat his vegetables. He still may not love them, but the more he is exposed to healthy foods, the more likely it is that he will develop good eating habits as he ages. As a parent, I cannot simply leave him to his natural cravings. Instead, I must work to help develop his taste for items that are good for him.

In a similar way, our cravings and desires for worldly items come quite naturally to us. Most of us could easily plop ourselves into a life full of respect, family, fame, fortune and friends, just as John easily plopped his face into his cupcake. However, desserts are for savoring, and they must never be mistaken for the real meal. We should enjoy the gifts and pleasures that the Lord brings into our lives, but we should never mistakenly believe that they are our sustaining power. As Thomas à Kempis aptly states, 'You cannot find complete satisfaction in any temporal gift, because you were not created to find your delight in them. Even if you possessed all the good things God has created, you could not feel happy and glad; all your gladness and happiness rest in the God who created those things.'[1] Part of spiritual growth is learning to feast on Christ, appreciating Him as our true meal and savoring time in His presence. Just as it will take time for my son John to learn to love healthy foods, it takes each soul time to grow up in Christ and learn to 'taste and see that the Lord is good.'[2]

This chapter focuses on an important goal for Christians: the cultivation of a desire and hunger for the Lord that will break the negative pattern of seeing, coveting, taking and hiding. It is possible to escape from the pattern that ensnared Eve and Achan, but such an escape will not simply

1 Thomas à Kempis, *The Imitation of Christ* Book 3, Chapter 16 (London: Fontana Books, 1963) p. 136.

2 Psalm 34:8

come about by an act of will power. If it were easy to change our desires, we would all be exercising five times a week and eating meals full of fruits and vegetables. Change in any area is neither easy nor quick. It will take time to turn our eyes from the temporal pleasures of this world and learn to desire the things of God. This change cannot be accomplished in our own power. In fact, a new power must be at work in our hearts if we are to escape from the mold of our worldly self and live as a new creation.

To help us take hold of this external strength, we will begin by looking at the temptation of Christ and observing His ability to break the pattern of sin that Eve and Achan succumbed to in their situations. Next, we will seek to understand the extent of His power at work in our lives as Christians. Lastly, we will look at a new pattern of belief that we can put on to replace the old pattern of unfaithfulness and sin.

Christ: The Pattern Breaker

In his gospel, Matthew gives an account of the temptation of Christ.[3] We are told that the Spirit led Jesus into the desert for the express purpose of temptation by the devil. Jesus fasted for forty days and nights, and then Satan came to him with three temptations. As we look at this account, we will consider the circumstances surrounding Christ's temptation, the nature of the temptations themselves and the method Christ used to fight the attacks of Satan. As we consider each category, we will contrast and compare His situation with that of Eve and Achan. Where they failed, Christ found success. Our goal is to understand His triumph so that we may emulate His method in our own battles with temptation.

Circumstances surrounding Christ's temptation

Satan came to Eve when she was surrounded by the perfection of the Garden of Eden. Her nature was not yet marred

3 Matthew 4:1-11

by sin, and she was enveloped by goodness on every side. Covetous desires came to Achan in the midst of great success in battle. While his nature was certainly impaired by sin, he was living in an era of Israelite history that witnessed the earthly fulfillment of God's promises to Abraham. He was entering into the hope of every Israelite for over four hundred years – the Promised Land. In contrast, Christ's temptation took place in extremely unfavorable circumstances. Instead of the perfection of the Garden of Eden or the hope of the Promised Land, Jesus' temptation took place in the wilderness. Rather than a cultivated Garden or a land flowing with milk and honey, the Spirit led Christ to a place of harshness and discomfort.

Both Eve and Achan also had the blessing of companionship as they faced temptation. Eve could have sought strength from Adam in her battle with Satan. Achan was surrounded by other warriors and could have gained strength in their fellowship and the example of their obedience. In contrast, Christ was alone for forty days and devoid of any human fellowship or comfort.

Lastly, fasting for forty days and forty nights would certainly have led to a weakened physical state for Christ as He faced Satan's temptation. His frame was fully human and in need of physical sustenance. Compare His situation with Eve, who was surrounded by the bounty of Eden, or Achan, who was enjoying the produce of Canaan.[4] All in all, Christ was lacking the comforts of home, companionship and basic physical needs as He faced the tempter.

Jesus' triumph in temptation while in weakness should lead each of us to realize that we are without the excuse of difficult circumstances in our own temptations. Often our covetous desires can lead us to believe in the uniqueness of our own situation. They secretly whisper that no one has ever faced such a struggle or felt the weight of our particular

---

4 Joshua 5:12

trial. However, Paul speaks to the falsehood of these lies in 1 Corinthians when he writes, 'No temptation has overtaken you that is not common to man.'[5] Whatever covetous desires you are facing, they are *common* to man. Lust, envy and greed come to each of us in many different forms, often when we find ourselves in difficult circumstances. However, we recall that Eve and Achan disobeyed because of their inner disbelief, not their outward circumstances. As we move through each of Christ's temptations, we will see that He triumphed because of His inner belief, in spite of the harshness of His circumstances.

The nature of Christ's temptation

Satan tempts Jesus in three ways. First of all, he tempts Him to prove He is the Son of God by turning stones into bread. Secondly, he asks Jesus to throw Himself off the temple to prove He is the Son of God, knowing that the angels will come to protect His fall. Thirdly, he tempts Jesus with all the kingdoms of the world and their splendor if He will simply bow down and worship Satan. These temptations were not haphazard choices on Satan's part, but intentionally chosen to tempt Christ in particular areas. Although Satan was tempting Christ to do physical acts (i.e. turn stone to bread), the real power behind the temptation was spiritual. Matthew Henry highlights the spiritual nature of these temptations by summarizing that Satan was seeking to tempt Jesus in the following three areas: '1. To despair of his Father's goodness. 2. To presume upon his Father's power. 3. To alienate his Father's honor, by giving it to Satan.'[6]

Observe how similar these temptations were to those Eve faced in the Garden. Her desire to eat from the tree was aroused by Satan's attack on God's goodness and power, as

5 1 Corinthians 10:13

6 Matthew Henry, *Matthew Henry's Commentary on the Whole Bible*, Volume 5, p. 26.

well as his whisperings that if Eve would take of the fruit she would be like God – an attack on His glory and honor. While we do not know the exact nature of Achan's temptation, we can easily understand that his coveting would first begin with a mistrust of God's goodness. He doubted the power of God when he believed that he could hide his actions and not be discovered. Similarly, he alienated God's honor by stealing items intended for God's temple and taking them as his own.

Satan will use similar attacks with each of us. He will tempt us to believe that God is holding back His goodness. He will come to us in our areas of weakness, being watchful to understand our desires, and he will attack. He will not fight honorably, as in some sort of knightly duel. He will fight with every evil intention and use every method of foul play. He roams and waits, looking for someone to devour.[7] His hope, and ultimate end, is to steal, kill and destroy.[8] We must understand the evil one's intentions if we are to fight the seductive nature of his temptations. His watchfulness met with his spite when he came to Jesus and tempted Him with bread after forty days of fasting.

Satan then continued his purposeful plan by tempting Jesus to presume upon God's power by using Scripture in a misleading way. He encourages the same licentiousness in many forms with us. He will tempt us to presume upon God's grace by speaking lies such as, 'The Bible says God is forgiving, so just do whatever you want.' He tempts us to presume upon God's love by questioning 'If God is loving, wouldn't He want you to have the item you desire?' He basically tempts each of us to take God's Word and twist it just enough to say exactly what we want to hear.

Lastly, Satan moves from the subtle to the overt when he tempts Christ with exactly what He came to receive.

---

7 1 Peter 5:8

8 John 10:10

Christ came to redeem a people for Himself and reign over an eternal kingdom. He rightly desired for the kingdoms of the world to be His possession. However, here Satan offers Jesus the kingdoms of the world without the pain of the cross. He tempts Christ to use wrong means (worship of Satan) to gain a right end. In a similar way, Satan will tempt each of us to believe that we should go after what we rightly desire without taking heed of the method we use. He patiently watches and observes our desires and offers them to us in sinful ways that would deprive God of the worship that comes from our humble obedience.

Christ's method of fighting temptation

In the account of Christ's temptation, Satan uses his usual schemes and methods in his attempts to cause Jesus to fall into the same pattern as our first father, Adam. While the nature of the temptation is similar, the end result is completely different. Satan is unable to penetrate the armor of Christ. With each temptation comes the rebuttal from Christ, 'It is written.'[9] He gives the following three replies:

> Jesus answered, 'It is written: "Man does not live on bread alone, but on every word that comes from the mouth of God."'[10]
>
> Jesus answered him, 'It is also written: "Do not put the Lord your God to the test."'[11]
>
> Jesus said to him, 'Away from me, Satan! For it is written: "Worship the Lord your God, and serve him only."'[12]

Christ fights the lies of Satan with the truth of the Scriptures. However, Christ does not simply know the

---

9 Matthew 4:1-11

10 Matthew 4:4

11 Matthew 4:7

12 Matthew 4:10

Scriptures, He *understands* and *believes* them. One can memorize many verses without ever believing what they contain or understanding what they mean. If we desire to fight Satan's attacks, we must immerse ourselves into God's Word and seek to understand the full counsel of the Bible. Simply attempting to memorize a few verses will leave us open for attack from the enemy. As shown in his advance against Jesus, Satan also knows the words of the Bible, and he will twist them in his attempt to entice us to sin.

From this account we should have a renewed understanding of the nature of our obedience. Obedience does not come about because of perfect circumstances, companionship or even our basic needs being met. Obedience springs from the well of belief. Christ's belief in God and desire for His Father's glory led Him to lead a perfect, sinless life. If we want to put off the old pattern of seeing, coveting, taking and hiding, we must put on belief and grow in our love and affection for the Father. In order to understand how Christ's obedience affects our ability to obey, we must look to the cross.

The Cross: A New Power Over an Old Pattern

The cross of Christ is the source of power in the life of a Christian. In order to understand this external strength, we must consider Christ's obedience, His death and resurrection, and the promises of His power given to all who believe. To begin with, Christ's obedience affects the Christian in two primary ways. First of all, His perfect life allowed Him to serve as atonement for our sins. In a sense, every Christian is actually saved by works – just not his own. We are saved by the perfect work and obedience of Christ. God's mercy towards the believer comes because Christ paid the debt of our sin through His death on the cross. He earned eternal life because of His perfect life. Yet, He bore and suffered death to take on the punishment we had earned through our sin. Secondly, Christ's obedience affects the Christian by giving us a new pattern to follow. His life shows forth what life in the Spirit looks like. He is the embodiment of the law lived out in the flesh. He is the 'word become flesh' and the model for our new life by the Spirit.[13]

While Christ's obedient life allowed Him to atone for our sins and illustrates a new pattern, it is His death and resurrection that gives us the power to live life in the Spirit. Christ's death gives us victory in two areas. First of all, His death gives us freedom from the *penalty* of sin. From the book of Romans we know that all have sinned and fallen short of the glory of God.[14] Each of us is rightly condemned to death as the penalty for our sins. However, Paul tells us that for all who believe, '[Jesus] was delivered over to death for our sins and was raised to life for our justification. Therefore, since we have been justified through faith, we have peace with God through our Lord Jesus Christ, through whom we have gained access by faith into this grace in which we now stand.'[15] We no longer need the blood of bulls and goats in order to approach a Holy God. Christ's blood atoned once for all and obtained our place in the family of God. Our penalty is paid in full, and we can live life free from the fear of eternal punishment.

Secondly, Christ's death gives us victory over the *power* of sin at work in our lives. Often we spend a great deal of time discussing the good news of Christ's work over the penalty, and we stop there. We need to realize and take hold of the good news that Christ's death and resurrection frees us from the power of sin in our lives today. Paul continues in Romans 8, stating, 'You, however, are controlled not by the sinful nature, but by the Spirit, if the Spirit of God lives

---

13 John 1:14

14 Romans 3:23

15 Romans 4:24–5:2

in you.'[16] Once we come to faith in Christ, we have a new power living inside us – the Holy Spirit. It is in His power that we are more than conquerors. It is in His power that we can fight the attacks of Satan. It is in His power that we can begin to hunger and thirst for righteousness instead of the temporal pleasures of this world. The power of the Holy Spirit in us gives life to our flesh and allows us to live as instruments of righteousness. We increasingly become what we were always created to be – image bearers of God – as we look more and more like Jesus. Our obedience follows His example and is by His power. Thus, He receives all the glory.

This power residing within us is talked about in great detail in the New Testament Epistles. Paul prays, asking that out of God's glorious riches He would, 'strengthen you with *power* through his Spirit in your inner being, so that Christ may dwell in your hearts through faith. And I pray that you, being rooted and established in love, may have *power*, together with all the saints, to grasp how wide and long and high and deep is the love of Christ, and to know this love that surpasses knowledge – that you may be filled to the measure of all the fullness of God.'[17] It takes God's power residing in us for us to even begin to understand the depth of love the Lord has for us. Similarly, Paul prays that the Colossians would 'live a life worthy of the Lord and may please him in every way: bearing fruit in every good work, growing in the knowledge of God, being strengthened with all *power* according to his glorious might so that you may have great endurance and patience, and joyfully giving thanks to the Father, who has qualified you to share in the inheritance of the saints in the kingdom of light.'[18] The Holy Spirit within us allows us to have great endurance, patience

---

16 Romans 8:9

17 Ephesians 3:14-19, emphasis mine.

18 Colossians 1:10–12, emphasis mine.

and joy as we live in our places of longing and waiting. We do not have to muster up the power within ourselves to endure patiently; God puts His own strength in our feeble jars of clay. When we are devoid of our own resources and abilities, it shines forth even more clearly that this power is from God and not from ourselves.[19] Living a contented, joyful life can only come from Christ's power at work in our hearts.

Christ's power inside our hearts also allows us to do more than we ever thought we could do. In Ephesians, Paul claims this strength when he proclaims, 'Now to him who is able to do immeasurably more than all we ask or imagine, according to his *power* that is at work within us, to him be glory in the church and in Christ Jesus throughout all generations, for ever and ever! Amen.'[20] The power of Christ – that resisted Satan, bore all your sins at Calvary and rose again on the third day – lives in you. While your flesh is weak, the Spirit of Christ lives within you and will strengthen you in every way for every work you are given to do. Peter asserts this truth when he states, 'His divine *power* has given us everything we need for life and godliness through our knowledge of him who called us by his own glory and goodness. Through these he has given us his very great and precious promises, so that through them you may participate in the divine nature and escape the corruption in the world caused by evil desires.'[21] This verse proclaims freedom from our covetous desires. Christ's power at work in us affords us everything we need for life and godliness. We are no longer forced to follow the pattern that Eve chose in the Garden. We are freed from the pattern of seeing, coveting, taking and hiding. Though the world is full of

---

19 2 Corinthians 4:7

20 Ephesians 3:20, emphasis mine.

21 2 Peter 1:3-4, emphasis mine.

corruption, we have everything we need at any moment to make the choice to obey.

Lastly, God's power within us allows us to overflow with hope. Satan will often try to convince us that whatever situation we are in, ultimately it is one without hope. Paul again turns to prayer and asks, 'May the God of hope fill you with all joy and peace as you trust in him, so that you may overflow with hope by the *power* of the Holy Spirit.'[22] Our joy, peace and hope do not flow from perfect circumstances or gaining all that this world has to offer. Instead, these items are fruits of spiritual growth. They are often born in the furnace of trials and afflictions, but they lead to a hope that is imperishable. God's power at work in us allows us to understand His love, live a life worthy of our calling, bear fruit in every good work, endure with patience, live a life of thanksgiving, escape the corruption caused by evil desires and finally, to overflow with hope. The gospel is not only good news for our eternal situation; it is also good news for our earthly situation. The way to abundant life can only be found in Christ.

THE CHRISTIAN: EXPERIENCING GOD'S POWER BY PUTTING ON A NEW PATTERN

As you read these verses, you may be wondering, 'If God's power does so much and has such effect, then what is my problem? Why do I feel enslaved to sin patterns? Why do I love watching TV more than reading my Bible? Why does sharing the gospel with someone make me feel so uncomfortable? Did I somehow miss out on this power when I came to Christ?' At times, true Christians are not marked by the obedience, peace and joy described in these verses. We suffer seasons of defeat, discouragement and spiritual dryness. Often, we continue to chase the pleasures of the world and simply approach Christianity as a nice

22 Romans 15:13, emphasis mine.

accompaniment to our life. If the secret to a contented and joyful life is Christ's power within us, we must learn how to take hold of and accept His strength within us.

To illustrate this concept (and it is a difficult one), I'll give you an example from my home. My car usually sits in the garage and is in full working order. It has good tires, a new battery and a full tank of gas. At times, my kids will stay in the car and play after we come home from being out. They love to sit in the front seat and pretend to drive and take trips. They change the radio station, move all the dials and go on many exciting imaginary adventures. I will sit in my kitchen, getting something accomplished and having no fear of them hurting themselves. While my car has the power to take them places, I know my children cannot take hold of that power. Why? They do not have the key to start the engine. The key that unlocks the power of the car sits safely on the table in front of me. The car has everything it needs to do all that it should do, but the designer of the car created a means to unlock that power. In a similar way, God has given means for us to grow in grace. We are being transformed into His likeness – it is a process of growth, not something that happens all at once.[23] This process, in theological terms, is known as 'sanctification'. Just as in justification (the declaration of righteousness that we receive when we become a Christian), sanctification is fully the work of God. Justification comes about through the appointed means of belief. In a similar way, sanctification comes about through belief. Belief is the key that opens up the power of the gospel at work in our lives. Our disobedience shows forth the areas where we do not believe and trust in the Lord. The inward belief of the Christian will well up within to produce outward actions and fruit. While it is fully God that sanctifies and changes us, this does not mean that we are passive in the process of sanctification.

23 2 Corinthians 3:18

Colossians 3 discusses the notion of actively removing our old ways of living and instead clothing ourselves with the virtues of Christ. To close this chapter, we will discuss in general how we can 'take off' the old pattern of seeing, coveting, taking and hiding and 'put on' a new pattern. Instead of seeing the things of the world, we will seek Christ. Instead of coveting, we will learn to *desire rightly*. Instead of taking, we will seek to *give generously*. Finally, instead of hiding, we will *confess* freely. As we put on this new pattern of belief – seeking the Lord, desiring rightly, giving generously and confessing freely – we will take hold of the means God has given us to allow His power to flourish in our lives. We will expand our understanding of this new pattern in the second half of the book, as we apply it to specific areas of desire. For now, we will consider these concepts only in an introductory way.

Seek the Lord instead of seeing

If we want to change our eating habits, we will never do so without a break from our old patterns. Rarely will one simply wake up and desire broccoli, squash, and peas after feeding for years upon ice cream, chips, fast food and pizza. At some point, we have to stop filling ourselves up with junk food in order to be hungry enough to enjoy that which is healthy for us. In a similar way, we must break from eating the world's goods if we want to be able to taste the sweetness of fellowship with the Lord. We must remove our gaze from the things of this world and start actively seeking the Lord. It is important to realize that our initial taste of time with the Lord might not feel as refreshing as watching TV, reading a gossip magazine or chatting with a friend. Similarly, healthy food might not initially taste as good to our tongues, but over weeks and years, as one observes the many benefits of healthy eating, it becomes apparent that our bodies work better and we get more enjoyment out of life when we make healthy choices. As a taste for healthy items increases, the appeal of unhealthy things loses its luster. Thus, as you consider the notion of seeking the Lord, keep in mind that time with Him will not change your desires in some sort of quick fix. However, over the course of months and years of daily pursuing God, you will see Him change your desires in such a way that your greatest desire becomes to know Him more because of the sweet satisfaction and joy found in Him.

Seeking after God begins with careful consideration of the way we spend our time. Most of us are filling our spare hours with something: extra work, movies, TV, Facebook, ministry opportunities, friends, exercise, or other enjoyments of some sort. None of these items are negative in themselves, but if they come at the expense of time with the Lord, then they have become idols in our lives. Making time to seek after the Lord will take thought and consideration on our part. We will have to remove obstacles to spending time with God. At different seasons of life, different pulls of the world invade our time with the Lord. Think through your life – what are you spending it on? What is filling up your life in such a way that it makes you sluggish in your pursuit of God? Whatever it is, it must be removed.

After considering what to take off, it is important to think about what needs to be put on in your pursuit of God. Pursuing God well involves being part of a church that is preaching God's Word. Hearing the goodness of the gospel preached each week is vital for our growth in the Lord. Being part of a church is more than just attending; it includes membership and regular participation in the sacraments. The sacraments of baptism and the Lord's Supper are the visual reminders of God's grace to us. In baptism, we remember that we come to Christ in weakness, needing to be cleansed. At the Lord's Supper, we remember that His body was broken and His blood was shed for us. The sacraments invite our senses to taste and see the goodness of the Lord. In addition to regular participation in worship, establishing fellowship within a Bible study or close group of friends will also encourage your relationship with God. Friends that help you know God's Word more, speak the truth in love and confront you when necessary are all part of pursuing God through the means of His church.

Lastly, our seeking after God must come with planned time alone with Him each day. We were created to need daily time for prayer and studying God's Word. However, in every season of life, Satan will convince us that we are just too busy to pursue God at that moment. We convince ourselves that once college is finished, work becomes manageable or the children are grown, we will take the time to sit quietly before the Lord. Or, we may convince ourselves that it is legalistic to try to pursue God everyday. We believe that we should only seek God when we 'feel' like it, or else we are being Pharisaical. Jesus never claimed that the Pharisees were legalistic in their active and devout pursuit of Himself. He claimed they were legalistic because they set up their own set of rules for righteousness. Is it legalistic to plan time with a friend or a spouse? No! We build and maintain friendships by careful planning and pursuit of the people we love. In the same way, we must carefully seek to spend time with the Lord if we want to grow in our relationship with Him and find the abundant life we are seeking.

We also must realize that we will not always leave our time with the Lord feeling more refreshed or more connected with the Lord. However, through months and years of faithful study, our time with the Lord will transform our minds and grow our enjoyment of God. A few years ago, some friends persuaded me to run a half-marathon with them. It took faithful planning and discipline, week after week. Many days I certainly did not feel like running. Some days I would have wonderful runs; enjoying the view and time with friends. Other days, it was a struggle just to make it around the block. If my feelings dictated my discipline in running, I never would have experienced the joy of finishing the race. In a similar way, if we want to grow in our affection for the Lord, we begin by seeking Him, in spite of how we feel on a particular day. In seeking the Lord we gain new eyes of faith that help us when the world comes calling with its various goods for us to 'see.'

Desiring rightly instead of coveting

Even as we grow in grace and faith, we will come to places of longing. The more we know the Lord, the more we start to long for good things. As mentioned in the first chapter, the Hebrew word for desire, *chamad*, also has positive meanings associated with it. One of the positive uses for the word comes when the Psalmist claims that God's Word is more to be desired than gold.[24] As followers of Christ, we should desire to know His Word and to understand it. The Bible also tells us that we should hunger and thirst after righteousness.[25] We should long to live our lives like Christ – to be His body, doing the Lord's will, until He returns. Coveting is an inordinate desire for something good or a culpable desire for something sinful. In contrast, we desire rightly when we long for God's work to be done, trusting Him in all that He withholds, and completely rejecting all that we know to be sinful. Thomas à Kempis describes this right desiring when he wisely counsels:

> So whatever desirable scheme presents itself to you, you must be governed by humility and the fear of God as you work towards it; above all, you must commit it entirely to [God], abandoning your own will, and saying: Lord, you know what is best. May your will decide what shall be done. Give what you will, how much you will, and when you will. Do what you know is best for me, do what pleases you and brings your name most honor. Put me where you will, and deal with me in all things as you please. I am in

24 Psalm 19:10

25 Matthew 5:6

> your hand – turn me backwards and forwards, turn me upside down. Here I am, your servant, ready for anything, for I have no desire to live for myself, but only to live perfectly and worthily for you.[26]

A right longing is always accompanied by a greater longing for God's glory, a desire for His will to be done and a trust that all His ways are better than what we could plan for ourselves.

In order to cultivate right longings in our hearts, we have to patiently consider what we are considering. By that, I simply mean taking the time to think through what we allow our minds to ponder throughout the day. It is easy to get in the habit of thinking upon the blessings of another's situation and grumbling about the negative circumstances we experience. It is tempting to focus on what we are waiting on God to accomplish instead of remembering all the past ways He has already displayed His faithfulness. We choose what we set our mind upon as we go about our day. We are called in Scripture to actively consider the love of the Lord,[27] to remember all He has done for us,[28] to consider how to spur one another on toward love and good deeds,[29] to consider it pure joy when we face trials of many kinds,[30] and to consider everything else a loss compared to the surpassing greatness of knowing Christ.[31]

E.B. Pusey, an Anglican pastor, gave the following guidelines for growing in contentment:

1. Allow thyself to complain of nothing, not even the weather.

---

26 à Kempis, *The Imitation of Christ*, Book 3 Chapter 15; 134.

27 Psalm 107:43

28 1 Samuel 12:24

29 Hebrews 10:24

30 James 1:2

31 Philippians 3:7

2. Never picture thyself to thyself under any circumstance in which thou are not.
3. Never compare thine own lot with that of another.
4. Never allow thyself to dwell on the wish that this or that had been, or were, otherwise than it was, or is. God Almighty loves thee better and more wisely than thou doest thyself.
5. Never dwell on the morrow. Remember that it is God's not thine. The heaviest part of sorrow often is to look forward to it. 'The Lord will provide.'[32]

As Christians, we are called to obedience not just in how we live, but also in what we think about. A mind that is set on considering these items will lead to a heart that wells up in contentment and belief.

Give generously instead of taking

A heart that is freed from the sin of coveting can give generously instead of taking. When we seek the Lord and desire rightly, the natural outcome will be a heart that gives generously. When our minds are set on the bounty that has been given to us in Christ, we are freed to love others, even at our own expense. Rather than look over the fence believing the grass is greener, we look over our neighbor's fence hoping to love and care for them the way Christ has cared for us. We give of our time, money, hope, support, encouragement, praise, love, prayers and energy with a new generosity of spirit because we know all of these are provided fully for us in Christ. We can give freely without fear because we trust fully that God sees all of our needs and will provide everything we need for life and godliness.

However, this new ability to give generously does not always come without pain. Just as Christ's work on the cross

32 Elisabeth Elliot, *Secure in the Everlasting Arms* (Grand Rapids, Baker: 2009), p. 136.

for our sakes brought Him suffering and death, our work at loving others with His generosity will at times come at great personal cost. We forgive when it hurts to forgive. We choose to love even the person who has wronged us. We seek peace when others seek revenge. Even in the furnace of persecution and affliction, a heart that believes God and desires His kingdom can give to others. Just as our sin of taking had negative ripple effects into our personal life, our family, our community and God's glory, so can our generous giving have multiple positive effects. One act of self-sacrificing generosity can have great impact for God's glory, His people, your family and your own life. Our belief in God's character and goodness allows us to become people who give in a Christ-like manner.

Confess freely instead of hiding

Lastly, in our quest for a new pattern of belief, we need to become people who confess freely instead of hiding. Achan and Eve both attempted to hide their sin against God. In Christ, we can come out of hiding and confess to the Lord and to those we trust. James exhorts us to 'confess your sins to each other and pray for each other so that you will be healed. The prayer of a righteous man is powerful and effective.'[33] We do not have to fearfully hide our imperfections from those around us, but instead we can confess and ask for help so that we may be healed. When we find that our desires have reached a sinful point, we should seek out a close friend and ask for prayer.

In a similar way, Hebrews encourages us to 'approach the throne of grace with confidence, so that we may receive mercy and find grace to help us in our time of need,' because we have a high priest (Christ) who has been tempted in every way, yet was without sin.[34] Thus, Christ can sympathize

33 James 5:16

34 Hebrews 4:14-16

with us in each and every temptation. He understands our struggles and can intercede and provide mercy and grace to help us. Also, we have the promise of John that 'if we confess our sins, he is faithful and just and will forgive us our sins and purify us from all unrighteousness.'[35]

In the Garden, Adam and Eve dressed in fig leaves to hide from one another and hid among the trees of the Garden to hide from the Lord. When faced with our sin, we are often tempted to hide from both God and others. As we put on the new pattern of belief, we can come out of hiding and live in the freedom of forgiveness. Christ's perfect obedience in His temptations is given to us through His death and resurrection. Through belief we possess the power within to turn from our old pattern of seeing, coveting, taking and hiding and walk in the new way of seeking the Lord, desiring rightly, giving generously and confessing freely. It is this new pattern of belief that is the secret of the contented heart.

Questions for Personal Reflection and Group Discussion

1. Can you think of a time when you cultivated a desire for something good? It could be healthier eating or exercise habits, better use of time or money, or any other way you have attempted to change your desires. How did you go about making these changes? How successful were you at changing your desires?

   Read Matthew 4:1-11

2. What were the circumstances surrounding Christ during His temptation? How do His circumstances compare to Eve's? Achan's? How do we tend to blame our sin on our circumstances?

35 1 John 1:9

3. How do you see Satan attacking God's goodness and power in this temptation?
4. How does Jesus resist temptation? What encouragement can you take from Christ's obedience in spite of His circumstances? What do you learn from His example?
5. How does Satan attack us with lies about God today? What are ways that he would want you to believe that God is not good or not powerful enough for your situation?
6. What does it mean to say that the cross of Christ gives us freedom from both the *penalty* of sin and the *power* of sin?
7. Read the following verses, noting the effect of Christ's *power* in the life of a Christian.
   a. Ephesians 3:14-19
   b. Colossians 1:10-12
   c. Ephesians 3:20
   d. 2 Peter 1:3-4
   e. Romans 15:13
8. Which of these verses about Christ's power at work in your life particularly gives you hope?
9. If we seek to change our covetous patterns in our own strength, what will be the result?
10. The new pattern of belief begins when we seek the Lord. What are some ways we can seek the Lord in our everyday lives?
11. Secondly, we need to begin to desire rightly. What are good desires to long after? What scriptures help you to know what you should desire?

12. Reread E.B. Pusey's guidelines for growing in contentment. Which of these would help you most to grow in your trust of what the Lord is doing in your life?
13. What are ways (not just monetary) that you could practice the grace of giving to others?
14. Read James 5:16, Hebrews 4:14-16 and 1 John 1:9. What are the benefits and blessings of confession?
15. Read over the following steps for growing in contentment from Elisabeth Elliot.[36] Which of these areas strikes you as a particularly helpful means of growing in contentment?

Growing in Contentment

1. Go to God first. Kneel in silence. Lift up your heart and hands. Listen. 'I am ready; let him do to me whatever seems good to him' (2 Sam. 15:26).
2. Receive the Givens and the Not-Givens. 'Lord, you have assigned me my portion and my cup; you have made my lot secure' (Ps. 16:5).
3. In acceptance lies peace. 'Peace I leave with you; my peace I give you. I do not give to you as the world gives. Do not let your hearts be troubled and do not be afraid' (John 14:27).
4. It is always possible to do the will of God. 'If you love me, you will obey what I command' (John 14:15, 15:10).
5. Do it now. 'I will hasten and not delay to obey your commands' (Ps. 119:60). 'You do not even know what will happen tomorrow' (James 4:14).

36 The following is taken from Elliot, *Secure in the Everlasting Arms*, pp. 120-1.

6. Love means sacrifice. 'This is how we know what love is: Jesus Christ laid down his life for us. And we ought to lay down our lives for our brothers' (1 John 3:16).
7. Choose your attitude. 'Your attitude should be the same as that of Christ Jesus, who...made himself nothing, taking the very nature of a servant...He humbled himself' (Phil. 2:5, 7-8).
8. Analyze your struggle. Is it merely delayed obedience? 'I run in the path of your commands, for you have set my heart free' (Ps. 119:32).
9. Give it all to Jesus. 'Whoever wants to save his life will lose it, but whoever loses his life for me will find it' (Matt. 16:25).
10. Do the next thing. 'In the evening my wife died. The next morning I did as I had been commanded' (Ezek. 24:18).
11. Give thanks every day and for everything. 'Always giving thanks to God the Father for everything' (Eph. 5:20). 'Let a righteous man strike me – it is a kindness; let him rebuke me – it is oil on my head. My head will not refuse it' (Ps. 141:5).

5 *Coveting Money and Possessions*

Now why is the devil's money accepted, the world's offer embraced, and God's rejected? Truly, men do not know the worth of what God offers them. The money the devil and the world offer is in their own currency, and is familiar to them. Swine trample on pearls, because they do not know their value. Men prefer the poor things they have because they are in their present possession. The devil seeks to peck out the eyes of men, that they do not see the blessed God and the happiness that is to be enjoyed in him. O how dull is the world's glass in the presence of true crystal! The magnet of earth will not draw man's affections while heaven is visible. He that has fed on the heavenly banquet cannot savor anything else.

George Swinnock

Voices From the Past, p. 257.

5

Coveting Money and Possessions:

The Story of Judas

A couple of years ago, at Reformed Theological Seminary's Women's Conference in Charlotte, I had the pleasure of hearing Elsie Newell speak. She spoke about her love for God's Word and the importance of it in our lives. At one point in her talks, she related how, years ago, she had promised her adult children and their spouses two thousand dollars each if they would memorize the Sermon on the Mount. This passage includes three full chapters from the Gospel of Matthew, totaling ninety-nine verses altogether. As I thought about it, I knew I would be very willing to memorize those verses if someone were paying me that amount of money. It began to disturb me, because I realized that it exposed something amiss in my own heart. If I was eager to memorize Scripture because I was being paid, instead of just wanting to memorize it because I believed it was good in itself, then I actually treasured what money could certainly provide over what I believed God's Word residing in my heart could provide. Of course, in my mind I believed God's Word was more of a blessing than money, but I realized how subtly and easily money could slip on the throne in my heart and become my motivating desire. One of my favorite passages in Scripture is Psalm 19:

> The law of the LORD is perfect, reviving the soul. The statutes of the LORD are trustworthy, making wise the simple. The precepts of the LORD are right, giving joy to the heart. The commands of the LORD are radiant, giving light to the eyes. The fear of the LORD is pure, enduring forever. The ordinances of the LORD are sure and altogether righteous. They are more precious than gold, than much pure gold; they are sweeter than honey, than honey from the comb.[1]

This passage relates so clearly the loveliness of God's Word – it revives the heart, makes wise the simple, gives joy to the heart, gives light to the eyes and is worth *much more* than pure gold. If God's Word has these many benefits, and is worth much more than money, then why would money motivate me to hide God's Word in my heart? Unfortunately, this response reveals an underlying incorrect belief that money is what revives the soul, gives joy to the heart and makes wise the simple. Even though I do not consider myself someone who is drawn to the pursuit of money or the love of it, here I found residing in my own heart the tendency towards the belief that it could certainly provide for me what God, through Jesus and His Word, only *might* provide for me. I never would have said that I want money in my pocket more than God's Word in my heart, but God was faithful to expose the inner belief of my heart.

The covetous desire for money or possessions is often called greed. Usually, I associate this term with a person who will do anything for money. In movies, greedy people connive, steal and murder in their pursuit of money. As we attempt to uncover and fight the greed residing in our own heart, we will need to take off those lenses. While we may not murder and plot in an attempt to gain money or

1 Psalm 19:7-10

possessions, at the heart of a greedy person is the belief that money itself is the provider instead of a means of God's provision. Different people believe different truths about money, but here are some to consider:

Money = Security
Money = Happiness
Money = Relational Peace
Money = Comfort
Money = Respect
Money = Pleasure
Money = Experiences
Money = Possessions
Money = Reward

Take a moment to read over that list. In your own experience, which of those speak to your heart? Do you believe that more money would make your relationship with your husband easier? Would money allow you to have more exciting experiences in life? Would it bring you comfort and ease so that you could work less and enjoy life more? Would it allow you to purchase more possessions that you believe would give you joy?

What if we exchange 'Money' for 'Knowing God'?

Knowing God = Security
Knowing God = Happiness
Knowing God = Relational Peace
Knowing God = Comfort
Knowing God = Respect
Knowing God = Pleasure
Knowing God = Experiences
Knowing God = Possessions
Knowing God = Reward

When you compare the two lists, which do you really believe?

While God may use the means of money in order to provide some of the items desired above, we must be careful to see God as the true provider of our desires, not money.

The purpose of this chapter is to look into the covetous desire for money. In order to do so, we will study Judas, the disciple of Jesus, who succumbed to the false promises of money. We will also study the pattern that greed takes in our own heart and expose the negative consequences it brings. Finally, we will look to put on a new pattern of belief in God as the Provider in order to fight the greed residing in our hearts and live a life of blessing and generosity to those around us.

JUDAS: DISCIPLE OF JESUS, LOVER OF MONEY

We all know of Judas as the disciple who betrayed Jesus. What we often fail to think through is why he betrayed Jesus. Three accounts in Scripture give us good insight into the reasons for his betrayal: the story of Jesus being anointed by Mary at Bethany, Judas' subsequent conversation with the chief priests,[2] and Judas' reaction to the news that Jesus was condemned.[3]

The story of Jesus being anointed at Bethany is told in Matthew, Mark and John. The Gospels tell us that Jesus was eating dinner at the home of Simon when Mary came with an alabaster jar of expensive perfume and poured it on His head and feet, wiping His feet with her hair. John tells us that Judas in particular objected to this display by asking, 'Why wasn't this perfume sold and the money given to the poor? It was worth a year's wages.'[4] While this reaction may have seemed noble, John continues, '[Judas] did not say this because he cared about the poor but because he was a thief; as keeper of the money bag, he used to help himself to what was put into it.'[5]

Here, we begin to see the first inklings of the root of Judas' betrayal. It was not simply hatred of Jesus that caused

---

2 Matthew 26:6-16; Mark 14:3-11; John 12:1-8

3 Matthew 27:3-5

4 John 12:5

5 John 12:6

his betrayal; it was a love of money. Perhaps Judas was living under the misguided assumption that he could love money and follow Jesus. However, in truth, Judas maintained an outward association with Jesus only as long as it supported his inward affection for money. This causes me to wonder if Jesus was speaking specifically to Judas, calling him to Himself, when He earlier warned, 'No one can serve two masters. Either he will hate the one and love the other, or he will be devoted to the one and despise the other. You cannot serve both God and money.'[6]

This outward association with Jesus most likely served him well as keeper of the moneybag throughout his years as a disciple. However, this incident – a grand waste of a year's wages in his accounting – pushed Judas over the edge. The love of one master caused hatred for the other. Just afterward, Judas left and went to meet with the chief priests, asking, 'What will you give me if I deliver him over to you?' Judas' inward affection for money finally won out and stripped him of his willingness to associate with Jesus. Thirty silver pieces were enough to allow Judas to betray all that he had seen and heard. Judas witnessed first-hand the feeding of the five thousand, Jesus walking on the water, the healing of the blind man, the cleansing of a leper, and the raising of Lazarus from the dead. His eyes had seen the coming of the Kingdom of God, yet his heart did not believe.

From this point on, Judas planned for an opportunity to betray Jesus. He patiently ate the Last Supper, allowed Jesus to wash his feet, and then at Jesus' own command, went out to accomplish his mission. He returned with a large crowd, armed with swords and clubs, sent from the chief priests. Judas himself was only armed with a kiss. The symbol of love instead became the signal of arrest. His last interaction with Jesus was full of intimacy, but completely lacking in affection.[7]

---

6 Matthew 6:24

7 Matthew 26:21-50; Mark 14:18-46; Luke 22:21-48; John 13:21-30, 18:2-18

However, Judas was unable to enjoy his thirty silver coins. Once he realized that Jesus was condemned, he was full of remorse and changed his mind. He came back to the chief priest and elders and stated, 'I have sinned, for I have betrayed innocent blood.' Instead of the mercy and grace he might have found with Jesus, he only found himself condemned by their reply, 'What is that to us? That's your responsibility'. Just like Achan, he was unable to enjoy his treacherous goods. He threw the silver into the temple and left, going away to hang himself. He could not live with what he had done and had no understanding of the forgiveness he might have laid claim to had he waited for the resurrection. His eyes did not see and his ears did not hear the good news that Jesus had proclaimed. His belief in money robbed him of the grace he may have found if he had only believed in Jesus.

Judas: The Pattern of Unbelief

In Judas' story, it is easy to see the pattern of unbelief and its resulting consequences. Judas' eyes began to focus on and see all that money could provide. What his eyes saw flowed to his heart, and he began to inwardly covet. At some point, he finally began to take from the moneybag. Perhaps he initially attempted to justify his behavior with thoughts such as, 'I'm not stealing; I'm just paying myself for the extra work of being in charge of the money.' Sin tends to cloak itself until it has full reign. Once it is fully master, then a person finds himself doing things he never thought he would do. Surely, Judas did not set out following Jesus with the intent to betray Him. However, his covetous desires were insatiable, so he continued farther and farther down the path of sin until he was willing to condemn a man whom he knew was innocent. However, all of his taking did not lead to satisfaction. It led to hiding. Judas hid his own love for money under a supposed love for the poor. While sitting at the table with Jesus, he even attempted to hide his betrayal with the denial, 'Surely not I, Rabbi?'[8] He had hidden himself so well that none of the other disciples could imagine who would betray Jesus. Even the betrayal itself was hidden in the guise of a kiss – a symbol of affection. Finally, when he realized the extent of his own treachery, he attempted to hide by giving the money back. However, nothing could undo what was done.

Judas: Painful Consequences

Judas' story, perhaps more than any other, speaks to the dire consequences our covetous desires can yield. He did not find satisfaction in this life, or in the next. Jesus himself tells us that Judas was lost, 'doomed to destruction'[9] and that, 'It would be better for him if he had not been born.'[10] It is one thing to face the consequences in this world, where we can also find forgiveness. It is another to face the consequence of an eternity without the saving mercies of Christ. Let me say clearly, Judas' love of money did not cause him to lose faith in Christ. Instead, Judas' love of money prevented him from ever truly believing in Christ. He walked with Him, but did not love Him or believe in Him. From his example, each of us should take great warning and examine our own hearts. When we simply have an association with God and His church, and do works of ministry, but are devoid of an active affection for Jesus, we leave ourselves open for other lovers to captivate and control our hearts. We can believe much about Jesus, without ever really believing *in* Him. If we are walking with Him, but devoid of love and affection, we may very well fall into the same destructive trap as Judas. Paul warns Timothy, 'People who want to get rich fall into temptation and a trap and into many foolish and harmful desires that plunge men into ruin and destruction. For the

---

8 Matthew 26:25

9 John 17:12

10 Matthew 26:24

love of money is a root of all kinds of evil. Some people, eager for money, have wandered from the faith and pierced themselves with many griefs.'[11] What we desire matters. It says something about what is happening in our hearts. A love of money exposes a lack of love for Christ. If you desire to be rich, be warned: Money is not an easy master and may one day fill your life with grief. If you want to find life, hear the words of Jesus: 'I have come that they may have life, and have it to the full.'[12]

The Pattern in Our Own Lives

To avoid the fate of Judas, we must first explore what a covetous pattern regarding money looks like in our own life. How does our seeing lead us to covet, take and hide? We also need to think about the consequences that result because of a wrong pursuit of money.

We See

We live in a world that allows us to see what is available for our consumption at almost every moment. Songs extol the value of money with lyrics such as, 'I want money, lots and lots of money'[13] and 'I wanna be a billionaire.'[14] Advertisements bombard our senses while we are on the computer, opening the mail, watching TV, driving in the car or even using a public restroom. With the Internet, it is now even easier to go from seeing something to buying it. An email is sent telling you of a sale with free shipping, and with just a couple of clicks and a credit card number, an item is purchased. There may have been no particular need for that item, but once the item was seen, it became a desire. Perhaps a catalogue is sent to your home with a perfect

---

11 1 Timothy 6:9-10

12 John 10:10

13 'I Wanna Be Rich' by Calloway.

14 'Billionaire' by Travis McCoy.

living room, and it sparks a longing in your heart. Surely your life would feel more peaceful and in control if you could just have a living room that felt more put together. Maybe a new coat would make you feel more attractive and people would like you more. Many times we have different root desires (control, respect, pleasing others, power) that spur our desire for money and possessions.

At times, it is the pervasiveness of advertising that wears us down. A single advertisement does not turn our head, but as we hear again and again of a particular item, we get worn down and start to believe that we truly need that scarf, camera, car, vacation, or new sofa. One Saturday morning, an infomercial for a product called the Swiffer Sweeper came on while I was upstairs drying my hair. All of a sudden, my two oldest children were running up to my room informing me of all the reasons we *needed* a Swiffer Sweeper. 'Mommy, Mommy, it picks up nails and tacks,' my son informed me. 'It also can be used on both hardwoods and the carpet,' my daughter told me. They both continued to run back and forth from listening to the infomercial to telling me verbatim how this new Swiffer Sweeper would change our lives. They promised that they would do all the cleaning up after dinner if they could just have this one item. Of course, I told them, 'No, we are not getting a Swiffer Sweeper.' I was not going to be sold by an infomercial. That evening, I related the story to a couple of friends who were over for a visit. One of the friends had actually purchased the Swiffer Sweeper and loved it. The other friend casually mentioned that she would really like to have one. By this point, I was sold. She and I went online and ordered them; my earlier resistance was completely worn down. Suddenly, I found myself purchasing the very item that I had told my children we did not need! While this purchase was not necessarily wrong, it does speak to how our seeing slowly makes us believe in the power of things to give our life fulfillment. For me, the recommendation of a friend was much more powerful than the infomercial. This example speaks to another common way our eyes begin to see.

While our eyes are often enticed by magazines, billboards or TV commercials, we can be equally and more persuasively drawn to items that our friends possess. If our neighbor buys a new minivan with the latest feature, all of a sudden ours seems very out of date. If our roommate comes home with the latest and greatest computer, our old one seems slower and more frustrating with every passing day. A friend starts shopping at a particular store, and all of a sudden, we feel the urge to just drop in and check it out. It is extremely difficult not to define 'normal' simply by what our friends possess. What the West defines as normal would be extreme luxury for almost anyone else in the world. We need to realize how often our eyes see what they want to see. We can be blind to those around us who have less, while fixating on those who have just a bit more.

It is important to note that simply seeing an advertisement or a friend's new home is not sin. We can see and enjoy the material blessings that God has given to a friend. However, we must be careful and understand our own weaknesses. If you struggle in this area, it may be time to call up certain companies and ask them not to send their catalogues to your home. For some, seeing clothing, furniture, books or travel magazines can stir up a sinful response. Each woman must know her particular areas of temptation and begin to fight by removing certain things from her view. Left unchecked, our seeing will become coveting.

We Covet Money & Possessions

There is a fine line between desiring and coveting. Once again, it comes back to the heart and is a matter of extent. Two women can want the exact same thing, and yet one is coveting, while the other is not. As it relates to money, there are some tell-tale signs that can help us uncover these covetous desires in our own heart.

First of all, if one is coveting money, she will compare herself with everyone around her. She spends her time thinking about another's income and the purchases she is making. She will know how much her friends spent on their houses, cars, clothes, computers and vacations. A greedy person will judge others for their monetary purchases, while always excusing her own purchases based on her circumstances. A covetous person keeps track and compares her own income with those around her.

Secondly, she will judge others based on their income. Those who are wealthy immediately have esteem in her eyes. She wants to become friends with those who have money, because they possess what she believes will make her happy. Yet, at the same time, she also judges those who have more money for the decisions they make. She will recognize their wasteful spending, while neglecting to look at her own purchases. She will think of all that they could give to the poor, while never feeling convicted of all that she has that she could share with others. In a sense, the covetous person both loves and hates people with money. She loves them because she wants to be them. She hates them because she is not them. Thus, coveting and judging go hand in hand. One leads to the other.

There are many other signs that show forth a covetous heart towards money. Complaining and grumbling about your income (or your husband's) displays a covetous heart. If money causes fights between you and your spouse or another family member, greed may be at the root of the problem. Being in debt or hoarding money are both signs that money is being viewed in an incorrect light. Lastly, I would encourage you to think about how you work when being paid versus work that you do to serve others or your family. Is money your greatest motivator? If you think you will get a larger bonus, do you work harder or encourage your husband to work harder? If our work is done for the Lord, that should be motivation enough for the Christian. As Hannah W. Smith states, 'And I am ashamed to think that any Christian should ever put on a long face and shed tears over doing a thing for Christ, which a worldly man would be only too glad to do for money.'[15] Christ should be the motivating factor in all our work and the money we are paid simply seen as His good provision for us. Once again, these are simply signs that a love of money may be reigning in our heart instead of a love for God. If our inordinate desires continue to grow, eventually they will bloom into a life of taking.

We Take

Our coveting leads to various forms of taking. We may actually steal from individuals or businesses in order to gain just a bit more. Most often, our taking comes in the form of what we fail to give to others who are in need. Our own frivolous spending habits greatly affect our ability to give generously to missionaries, those in need in our own congregation, and the poor. Many husbands take time, love and availability from their families as they pursue money. Many women also take time from their families in order to sustain a certain type of life-style they have come to enjoy. One can easily take joy away from a friend by coveting what the Lord has given her. Perhaps a friend goes on a vacation that we cannot afford, and rather than rejoice with her, we sit and complain about our own lack of resources. Our grumbling and complaining about God's provision takes glory from His Name as we fail to come before Him with a thankful heart.

We Hide

Once our seeing has led us to covet and our coveting to taking, we will then find ourselves in places of hiding. Judas hid

15 Hannah W. Smith, *The Christian's Secret of a Happy Life* (London: Nisbet, 1950), p. 189.

his own love of money under a guise of love for the poor. Many a husband hides his love for money under the right desire to care for his family. However, if his definition of provision is limited only to financial resources, then he will ultimately fail them, all the while convinced his pursuit is a good one. We hide stealing from our company's resources under the belief that they should be paying us more. We hide our failure to give to those in need by claiming that we were unaware, when in truth we were simply blinded by our own desires for more money. We can even attempt to hide our grumbling and complaining under the auspices of prayer requests and being honest and open with those around us.

We Bear Consequences

Ultimately, the pursuit of wealth will lead to dire consequences. As Ralph Waldo Emerson once said, 'Money often costs too much.' For the individual, loving money will never lead to satisfaction with life. As Solomon wisely warned, 'Whoever loves money never has enough; whoever loves wealth is never satisfied with his income.'[16] For the family, a love of money will lead to misplaced priorities, strife in marriage and discontented children. The community will suffer from the results of coveting as well. Missionaries will be delayed in getting to their field because of a lack of giving. The poor will suffer greatly, and some will even die because they lack the necessities for life. Both time and resources will be spent in the pursuit of money that might have gone to advance the Kingdom of God. Money also comes with the warning that it is a means of keeping people from faith. Paul tells us that people eager for money have wandered from the faith.[17] Jesus warned that it was difficult

---

16 Ecclesiastes 5:10

17 1 Timothy 6:10

for the rich to enter the kingdom of God.[18] In the parable of the seeds, Jesus equated the seed that fell among the thorns as the man who hears the Word, but the worries of this life and the *deceitfulness of wealth* choke it, making it unfruitful.[19] The desire for riches is particularly precarious for your soul. The greatest consequence a love of money can yield is a life of unbelief that never truly comes to know the saving message of the gospel. We will spend the last part of this chapter discussing how to fight against this assault on our faith by nurturing a love for God that expels all other inordinate desires from our heart.

Putting on a New Pattern: Seek the Lord

If we want to fight against this temptation to covet money and possessions, we will need to begin by seeking the Lord. There are two primary truths about God that directly relate to our view of money and possessions. The first is that God is our Provider. Paul exhorts Timothy to command the rich not to 'be arrogant nor to put their hope in wealth, which is so uncertain, but to put their hope in God, who richly provides us with everything for our enjoyment.'[20] Our hope for provision must be centered on God, not on our own works. While it is right to work with diligence and good to earn a wage, we must not see our own hard work or bank account as our hope. Instead, we need to view all that we have as God's provision for us. A person who believes in God as Provider prays and seeks counsel regarding purchases. She is thoughtful and wise with her money because she views it as entrusted to her by the Lord, rather than earned by her own work. She is also thankful, because her prayerful heart gives her eyes to see what has been provided instead of dwelling on what is lacking. When we rightly believe in

18 Mark 10:23

19 Matthew 13:22

20 1 Timothy 6:17

God as *Provider*, our eyes turn from self and look to God with expectation and trust. A God-centered view of money and possessions leads to a quietness of heart that allows us to say with Paul, 'I know what it is to be in need, and I know what it is to have plenty. I have learned the secret of being content in any and every situation, whether well fed or hungry, whether living in plenty or in want. I can do everything through him who gives me strength.'[21]

The second relevant truth about God is that He, in Himself, is our greatest reward. When God appears to Abram, He encourages him not to be afraid by stating, 'I am your shield, your very great reward.' The writer to the Hebrews encourages them to 'Keep your lives free from the love of money and be content with what you have, because God has said, "Never will I leave you; never will I forsake you."'[22] Our contentment flows from God's presence. If we have God, though we have nothing else, we have the one thing that matters. Christ's blood is worth more than all the kingdoms and riches in the world. If simple wealth would have satisfied our souls, then there was no need for Christ to die. God simply could have provided everyone with great riches. However, He knows our true desires will only be met in relationship with Jesus. His presence in our lives, knowing Him as our greatest reward, gives us contentment in all things. If you want to free yourself from a love of money, it begins by knowing, believing and worshipping God as your provider and great reward.

Desire Rightly

As we seek the Lord, we take off old desires and begin to long for right and better things than money. To begin to desire well, we must first take off two covetous tendencies: comparing and complaining. If we want to begin to set our

---

21 Philippians 4:10

22 Hebrews 13:5

affections on the goodness of God towards us, then we must stop comparing our lives with the lives of those around us. Yes, there will be people who have more than us. There will also be people who have less. Truthfully, neither matter at all. God knows *your* frame. He knows just the amount of riches and just the amount of poverty that your frame can bear. You need not compare your lot to those around you. If you are in Christ, you have the greatest riches imaginable. If He has given you His own Son, certainly He will give you all things.[23]

Secondly, we need to take off our tendency towards complaining. It is not wrong to share that you have a need, but it is sinful to grumble and complain about the Lord's provision. I can see clearly the difference between the two when my children ask for something. How different it is to hear, 'Mommy, may I please have a glass of juice?' instead of a loud whiny declaration, 'I am thirsty. Get me some juice.' One is a patient asking for provision, while the other is an entitled demand, stated with a heart of dissatisfaction. The best way to take off the tendency to complain is to put on thankfulness. Each day we must actively choose to see what God has provided. Once we begin to look at our life through these lenses and focus our eyes on His goodness to us, out of our hearts will flow thanksgiving instead of complaining. Our outward grumbling is a sure sign of inner coveting.

As we take off comparing and complaining, we will begin desiring in two new ways. First of all, we will desire to store up great treasure for ourselves. Jesus commanded his followers, 'Do not store up for yourselves treasures on earth, where moth and rust destroy, and where thieves break in and steal. But store up for yourselves treasures in heaven, where moth and rust do not destroy, and where thieves do not break in and steal. For where your treasure

23 Romans 8:32

is, there your heart will be also.'[24] We are actually called to store up treasures for ourselves, provided that they are heavenly ones. If we really believe heaven is where we will live for eternity, we should seek to have our lives defined by work for that kingdom, instead of temporal gains here that will not accompany us into the grave. This verse came to impact me greatly over the past couple of years as the economy took a hit because of the banking industry. I live in Charlotte, which is a banking center. Many people saw much of their savings disappear almost overnight. What seemed safe and sound in the bank was in many ways stolen as stock prices fell dramatically. It is a good thing to save money and invest wisely. However, we also must understand that wealth is fleeting and realize that what is here today might be gone tomorrow, through no fault of our own. In contrast, what we give to God's work can never be taken away. Our diligent labors, generous gifts of money, and heartfelt prayers are storing treasures in heaven that are fully secure. We should desire to build, labor and give more and more for *that* Kingdom, knowing that our work is not in vain.

A second shift will be our desire to be a steward instead of an owner. There is a great difference between the two. A steward is entrusted with the care of something until the true owner returns. An owner believes an item actually belongs to him. The Bible never speaks against ownership in this present world; it is part of living in a stable, functioning, civil system. In fact, the command, 'You shall not steal'[25] presupposes ownership. However, we need to realize that all that we have here will one day be passed on to someone else. In fact, many of the items we treasure may one day be sold at garage sales or on eBay. God provides items for us during our stay on this earth, but we do not truly own them. All that is on earth will remain on earth. We are simply stewards of

---

24 Matthew 6:19-21

25 Deuteronomy 5:19

these items which have been entrusted to us to use for God's glory. With that mindset, we seek to take care of our homes, cars and other possessions. We care for them because we want to please the Lord, not because we are fearful of losing money by neglecting them. Viewing all of our items as truly belonging to God helps us to avoid becoming possessed by our possessions. Instead, we can use and enjoy them with thanksgiving, knowing they are simply part of His goodness to us. In these ways, by taking off comparison and complaining and putting on a desire for true treasure and stewardship over our earthly possessions, our hearts begin to awaken to right desires and longings with regard to money.

GIVING GENEROUSLY

As we seek to put on a new pattern, one vital part in guarding our hearts regarding money is being willing to give it away. The Bible teaches us to give generously, freely and sacrificially. In the Old Testament, 1 Chronicles recounts David's great rejoicing because of the generous giving of the Israelites for God's temple. His joy is full of humility and true gratefulness as he says, 'But who am I, and who are my people, that we should be able to give as generously as this? Everything comes from you and we have given you only what comes from your hand.'[26] David rightly reflects upon the fact that the people are honored to be able to give to the Lord. His praise to the Lord is full of humility and has no hint of pride. When our hearts are properly focused on God, we will follow in David's example and consider ourselves blessed in our ability to give. All that we give to the Lord was already His. All that we give to others was first given to us by His loving hand. In the knowledge that we are cared for by a loving and gracious Provider, we should give generously.

In addition to giving generously, we should give freely. When we give to the work of the church and to others, there

26 1 Chronicles 29:14

should be no strings attached. We should not consider our pastors, missionaries or other church employees as receiving money from ourselves. Instead, they are provided for by God, who uses the means of tithes and offerings to pay them for their work. Similarly, God uses your employer to provide you with wages for your work. God provides for each, yet he uses different means. Thus, when your missionary friend or pastor takes a family vacation, you may be tempted to think, 'I guess my money is paying for their family to have a lot of fun.' In contrast, by giving freely you can rejoice with them, knowing that God provided for them and they are responsible to Him for their stewardship. Giving freely involves giving with the understanding that the use of the money is in God's hands.

Lastly, we should seek to give sacrificially. Jesus commended the widow who gave out of her poverty with the words, 'I tell you the truth, this poor widow has put more into the treasury than all the others.'[27] The manner in which we give is more important than the amount. While one may give many thousands of dollars, this person's gift may actually be less than that of the person who simply gives a penny out of her poverty. God is well aware of the sacrifice of your own giving. I encourage you to give in such a way that you feel the cost of it. It is good for your soul and will help you keep an eternal perspective. One simple way my husband and I have chosen to do this in our own family is to not purchase cable TV. Instead, that money goes specifically to a missionary family we support. Whenever I am tempted to wish we had cable, I am reminded that this family is living so far from home, without many comforts, in order to bring the gospel to people who never would have heard. All of a sudden, not having cable feels like a privilege! While I fully realize giving up cable is not a great sacrifice, I do encourage you to think through ways you can make small sacrifices

27 Mark 12:43

in order to give to others. It will refresh and encourage you and spur your heart on towards greater giving. It will also be a means of sharing with your children the blessing of giving to others. As we give generously, freely and sacrificially, money and possessions will lose further ground in our heart and we will experience the blessings that come from that freedom.

Confess Freely

Finally, if we want to fight against the inordinate desire for money, we will need to confess to others when we struggle with this sin. Each of us may struggle with a desire for money for different reasons. When we see it in our heart, we need to confess it to a friend or pastor, knowing the evil it can work if left unchecked. We need to take the time to consider how money is shaping our choices and desires and ask others if they see a pursuit of possessions ruling our lives. As part of our confession, we also need to be willing to make amends. If we have stolen from someone, we should repay. If we have failed to give, we should begin giving generously. Immediately upon coming to faith, Zacchaeus' view of money changed dramatically. He promised, 'Here and now, I give half of my possessions to the poor, and if I have cheated anybody out of anything, I will pay them back four times the amount.'[28] His love for Jesus instantly changed his desire for money. A heartfelt confession should be accompanied by true lifestyle change.

Blessings Abound

While many negative consequences flow from a belief in money, many blessings accompany belief in God as provider and great reward. When we take on this new pattern of belief, we work for a treasure that can never spoil or fade. One day, in heaven, we may joyfully meet people who

---

28 Luke 19:8

became Christians as a result of God's using the money we gave. Earthly lives here may be saved from perishing because of our generosity. We possess a new freedom towards our possessions and do not feel enslaved by them. Our soul is protected from a love of things because we worship God as the provider of all of our needs. Our children learn generosity and greater trust in God by observing our freedom to give. Most importantly, God is greatly glorified when we find life in Him and glory in His provision, whatever it may include.

If you struggle in this area, I encourage you to read a chapter by A.W. Tozer entitled 'The Blessedness of Possessing Nothing.'[29] He closes with the following prayer:

> Father, I want to know Thee, but my cowardly heart fears to give up its toys. I cannot part with them without inward bleeding, and I do not try to hide from Thee the terror of the parting. I come trembling, but I do come. Please root from my heart all those things which I have cherished so long and which have become a very part of my living self, so that Thou mayest enter and dwell there without a rival. Then shalt Thou make the place of Thy feet glorious. Then shall my heart have no need of the sun to shine in it, for Thyself wilt be the light of it, and there shall be no night there. In Jesus' name, Amen.

May his prayer be your own and may your heart have no rival, but be filled by Christ alone.

Questions for Personal Reflection and Group Discussion

1. Look at the list on page 121. For which of these do you tend to trust in money rather than in God? Why?
2. Read Matthew 26:6-16 and John 12:2-8. In these parallel accounts, what hints do you see that reveal Judas' love for money?

29 A.W. Tozer, *The Pursuit of God* (Camp Hill: Christian Publications,1982), p. 30.

3. How did Judas's love of money yield painful consequences? See John 17:12 and Matthew 26:24.

4. Read Matthew 6:24 and Matthew 13:22. While there are many things we can set our hearts upon and worship, why do you think Jesus specifically warns us against money? What makes money dangerous for so many?

5. Read 1Timothy 6:6-9. What principles about money can you take from this passage? Is it wrong to be wealthy? What does Paul warn against?

6. How does what we see affect our desire for more money? What are some ways advertisers encourage you to desire their products?

7. Why does a woman who covets money both love and hate those who have money? How do our desires in this area make us judgmental towards others and covetous towards others?

8. Read the quote from Hannah Smith on page 130. What would it look like for our work to be motivated by pleasing God instead of making money? Think through your areas of free service. Do you labor in those things with the same devotion that you labor when being paid a wage?

9. What are the ways our covetous desires for money lead us to take from those around us? How do we hide our sin in this area?

10. What truths do we need to understand about God in order to fight our greed? See 1 Timothy 6:17 and Hebrews 13:5.

11. In order to desire rightly, we need to stop comparing and complaining. How do comparing and complaining only lead to more coveting?

12. Read Matthew 6:19-21. How would it look for you to store up treasure in heaven, rather than on the earth? How would your life look different if you began living this way?

13. A. W. Tozer says, 'After that bitter and blessed experience I think the words "my" and "mine" never had again the same meaning for Abraham. The sense of possession which they connote was gone from his heart. Things had been cast out forever. They had now become external to the man. His inner heart was free from them. The world said, "Abraham is rich," but the aged patriarch only smiled. He could not explain it to them, but he knew that he owned nothing, that his real treasures were inward and eternal.'

    What is the difference between a steward and an owner? How does our belief about our possessions change our relationship to them?

14. How do you need to give more generously, freely and sacrificially? Read 1 Chronicles 29:14. How does David's attitude in giving compare to your own?

15. Read Luke 19:8. How did Zacchaeus' faith change his relationship to money? How should our faith change our relationship to money?

6 Coveting within Romantic Relationships

When sin rises to tempt, it always seeks to express itself in the extreme. Every unclean thought would be adultery if it could; every covetous desire would be oppression; and every thought of unbelief would be atheism. It is like the grave that is never satisfied. Sin's advance blinds the soul from seeing its drift from God. The soul becomes indifferent to sin as it continues to grow. The growth of sin has no boundaries but the utter denial of God and opposition to him. Sin proceeds higher by degrees; it hardens the heart as it advances. Mortification withers the root and strikes at the head of sin every hour. The best saints in the world are in danger of a fall if found negligent in this important duty.

JOHN OWEN

Voices From the Past, p. 53.

6

Coveting within Romantic Relationships:

The Story of David

Last week I went to see the Broadway musical *Wicked*. It is a retelling of the story *The Wizard of Oz* and recounts the relationship between Galinda (who becomes Glinda the Good Witch) and Elphaba (who becomes the Wicked Witch of the West) prior to Dorothy and Toto coming to Oz. It is witty and funny, and provides interesting insight into our desire for relationship. Both Galinda and Elphaba fall in love with the same man, Fiyero. Galinda schemes to coerce him into an engagement, even though she senses he is not in love with her. She sings to the crowd in an attempt to convince herself, 'So I couldn't be happier, because happy is what happens when all your dreams come true. Well isn't it? Happy is what happens when all your dreams come true!' She clings to the belief that getting what she wants relationally will ultimately bring her fulfillment and joy. On the other hand, Elphaba, born with bright green skin, feels completely unworthy of love. As she sings, she warns herself, 'Don't wish, don't start, wishing only wounds the heart. I wasn't born for the rose and the pearl. There's a girl I know, he loves her so. I'm not that girl.'

When it comes to desiring the intimacy of the marriage relationship, often we can vacillate between these two divergent beliefs. On one side, we believe that once Prince Charming comes into our life, riding in on his white horse, all our dreams will be fulfilled and that 'happy is what happens when all your dreams come true.' We can wrongly cling to the belief that once our dream of marriage comes true, happiness will follow. At other times, we pull back from relationships and warn ourselves, 'don't wish, don't start, wishing only wounds the heart.' In an effort to protect ourselves from hurt, we squelch desire altogether. It could be that we feel unlovable for some reason. Or, perhaps we do not want to be perceived as a woman desperate for a husband, so we push down our desire for that relationship. For whatever reason, we simply let go of desire, thinking to ourselves, 'I'm not that girl.'

As we begin, it is important to remind ourselves that we are created to be in intimate relationship with others. In the very beginning, God created the world and each day He observed that it was good. However, once He made Adam and put him in the Garden, we are told that the Lord said, 'It is *not good* for man to be alone. I will make a helper suitable for him' (emphasis added).[1] The first *not good* in all of human history happened before sin even entered the picture. God, a relational Creator, had created Adam in His own image. Thus, Adam had both a need and desire for relationship. In His goodness, God created Eve, a suitable helper, and declared all that He had made to be 'very good.'[2]

It is also important to remember that once sin entered the Garden, all of our relationships suffer from the effect of that brokenness. The peaceful harmony of our original sinless state was marred, and every marriage will suffer the consequences to some extent. In particular, one consequence of the fall for

---

1 Genesis 2:18

2 Genesis 1:31

the woman was, 'Your desire will be for your husband, and he will rule over you.' We would be highly naïve if we believe that 'happy is what happens' when our marital dreams come true. We need to bring our good and right desire for relationship together with an understanding that no earthly relationship can mend the brokenness in our lives.

We will spend the next two chapters discussing our desires for relationships. This chapter will deal primarily with the hope and longing for a husband and what happens when the desire for a romantic relationship becomes covetous. The next chapter will discuss our desires in familial relationships and friendships. Our good desire for affection becomes covetous when it grows inordinate or culpable. The term 'inordinate' speaks to the depth of desire, while 'culpability' speaks to desiring the wrong person. A woman with an inordinate desire will *do anything* in order to gain what she wants. A person with a culpable desire for relationship will *pursue anyone* in order to meet her desire for relationship. To gain insight, we will look at the story of David and Bathsheba and observe the covetous relational pattern that occurred and the harmful consequences that followed. We will consider the pattern this desire can take in our own lives, whether we are single or married. Finally, we will consider what we need to believe about God in order to desire rightly and hope well in our romantic relationships.

David and Bathsheba

The story of David and Bathsheba is one of the most well-known in all of Scripture. It illustrates in great detail the pattern a covetous desire for relationship can take, as well as the negative consequences that result. In their story, we are dealing primarily with the covetous desire usually referred to as *lust*. Like greed and envy, lust is a specific form of coveting. In Scripture, the term always refers to an incorrect desire for a sexual relationship. While their story deals with this specific form of relational desire, it also can give wisdom and warning for any of the inappropriate forms our relational desires can take.

David saw

The story begins as David remains in Jerusalem while his army goes out to war against the Ammonites.[3] One evening, David got up from his bed and walked around the roof of the palace. As he looked out upon the city, he *saw* a beautiful woman bathing. While it is true that not all of our seeing is sinful, it is important to note that in this instance the very act of seeing was wrong and most likely the opportunity for it came about as the result of incorrect choices. It would be one thing if the story told us that David simply glanced upon a woman bathing and quickly turned his eyes away. Instead, we are told that he had time to take in that she was beautiful. He must have watched her in such a way that was sinful in itself, causing him to lust after her. At this moment, he did not take upon himself the wisdom of Job, who declared, 'I made a covenant with my eyes not to look lustfully at a girl.'[4]

It is also important to note the opportunity for his observation. We are told that the entire Israelite army was out to war. David's men were living in tents, facing the reality of battle, yet he stayed in Jerusalem and enjoyed the comforts of his palace. Rather than fulfill his duty to be with his men in wartime, he found himself idly walking along the roof. As Matthew Henry notes, 'Idleness gives great advantage to the tempter. Standing waters gather filth. The bed of sloth often proves the bed of lust.'[5] John Owen similarly comments, 'The mind is drawn away from duty, and the affections are enticed unto sin.'[6] Part of avoiding

3 2 Samuel 11-12

4 Job 31:1

5 Henry, *Matthew Henry's Commentary on the Whole Bible*, Volume 2, p. 386

6 John Owen, *Overcoming Sin and Temptation*, (eds. Kelly Kapic and Justin Taylor; Wheaton: Crossway Books, 2006) p. 326.

inappropriate relationships is to actively follow God's call upon our life. Diligent performance of our duties may prevent the idleness that can afford our eyes opportunity to see and be tempted into sin. David gave himself the opportunity to see and did not turn his eyes or thoughts from Bathsheba's beauty. Instead, he observed her, and then sent someone to find out about her.

David coveted

The messenger came back with the report that the beautiful woman was Bathsheba, the wife of Uriah the Hittite. If there was any doubt as to whether David's seeing had become covetous, it quickly became apparent as he sent for her to come to him. His desire for relationship was culpable in nature because he was willing to pursue Bathsheba, even though he knew it was against the seventh commandment, 'You shall not commit adultery.'[7] Lust conceived in his mind laid the groundwork for all that would follow.

David took

In chapter one, we discussed the notion that coveting is a 'mother sin' in that it begets other sins. This principle is seen clearly as David's covetous desires snowball into adultery and murder. First, he takes Bathsheba and sleeps with her. She becomes pregnant and sends word to David. He then brings her husband, Uriah, home from the front lines with the hope that he will sleep with his wife and believe that the child is his own. When this original plan fails, David makes Uriah drunk in order to further entice him to forget his duty and go to his wife. It is important to note that Uriah was so loyal to God, Israel, his fellow soldiers and King David that he was unwilling to enjoy the comforts of his home while 'the ark and Israel and Judah are staying

7 Exodus 20:14

in tents.'[8] Uriah's faithfulness is striking in comparison to David's dereliction of duty. However, David's own heart was not stirred or convicted by Uriah's obedience. Instead, he sent Uriah back to the front carrying a letter to Joab that was his own death sentence. This letter instructed Joab to place Uriah near the front lines for the express reason that he would be killed in the fighting. Even though Uriah had proved his loyalty to Israel so completely, David still connived to plan his murder. David's desire for Bathsheba led him to commit adultery, encourage drunkenness, and murder one who had been completely faithful to him. He took drastic ways in order to fulfill his selfish pursuits.

David hid

Much of the sin in this story is perpetrated in David's attempt to hide his adulterous affair with Bathsheba. First of all, he tried to hide by encouraging Uriah to sleep with his wife so that he would falsely believe the baby was his own. When that plan failed, David hid his murder of Uriah as part of the casualties of war. He then married Bathsheba in hopes of hiding that he had impregnated her in an adulterous affair prior to their marriage. David's hiding led to further sin and more hiding. Perhaps he believed that he had gotten away with his crimes and that they would remain hidden. However, even though he had hidden his deeds from his people, he could not hide from God.

David suffered consequences

The Lord was not pleased with David and sent the prophet Nathan to him. Nathan came with a parable that awoke David to the heinous nature of his crimes, so that David confessed, 'I have sinned against the Lord.'[9] Although David repented of his behavior, Nathan still assured him that consequences

8 2 Samuel 11:11

9 2 Samuel 12:13

would follow. The baby that Bathsheba delivered would die. Calamity would come upon David as one of his own sons would fight him for the kingship and lie with all his wives in broad daylight. The sword would never depart from David's house. While Nathan spoke of the consequences, he also spoke of God's mercy by proclaiming, 'The LORD has taken away your sin. You are not going to die.'[10] Even though David was the king, he could not escape the consequences of his behavior, nor his own need for forgiveness. His wrongful desire for a good thing led him down a path of sin that bore consequences for generations.

David's story illustrates the pain that a culpable desire for relationship can yield. He also exemplifies how finally getting everything we want does not necessarily satisfy. David's life was at the pinnacle of success when he saw Bathsheba. He was king after years of being chased and pursued by Saul. His armies were successfully defeating their enemies. He had multiple wives for companionship, along with many children. He lived in a palace and had loyal commanders and subjects. In the midst of the most favorable circumstances, he still found himself with covetous desires. David had spent years trusting and obeying God in difficult circumstances, but struggled to believe and obey God when his circumstances were favorable. Often our difficulties force us to God in ways that make our affection grow, while ease allows for our trust and hope to become fixated on other people or things. As Owen aptly warns, 'Look to the vigor of the affections toward heavenly things. If they are not constantly attended, excited, directed and warned, they are apt to decay, and sin lies in wait to take every advantage against them.'[11] David's descent should warn each of us of our own capacity to become entangled in a web of sinful desires. In the following section, we will consider a variety

10 2 Samuel 12:10-14

11 Owen, *Overcoming Sin and Temptation*, p. 332.

of ways the pattern of seeing, coveting, taking and hiding takes hold in our own covetous desires for relationship.

The Pattern in Our Own Lives: We See

I remember distinctly one Sunday coming into church and sitting with my family; just in front of us was a married couple with a new baby. As they sang, the husband sweetly put his arm around his wife and smiled down at her. They looked so in love and happy with one another. In that instant, my seeing led me into doubts about my own marriage. Was I that happy? Did my husband love me the way her husband loved her? Why didn't my husband put his arm around me in church? What I saw caused me to begin to doubt what I knew to be true. In reality, I know that my husband loves me dearly, and I am thankful to be his wife. Yet, here I was becoming discouraged about my own marriage simply because of the affection being shown by another couple. Drawing conclusions about my own marriage based on one particular moment in someone else's relationship is neither wise nor helpful. Our vision of another's relationship is always limited to what we think we see. In truth, the reality of their situation is unknown to us. What we see (or think we see) relationally between others can cause all sorts of discontentment to spring up within our hearts. Whether single or married, widowed or divorced, we all see things we desire relationally. Our seeing can be divided into two areas: what we want to *have* and what we need to *become* in order to find satisfaction relationally.

We see many things we want to have relationally. We desire a husband who is tender and kind, yet also strong and confident. We want him to be able to fix the car, as well as cook up a nice dinner. We want him to share emotions without being too emotional, and to be successful without being prideful. Most of us could easily put together in our mind characteristics that would make the perfect mate. We choose specific qualities from different men we meet. We like this man's personality, another man's looks, another's sense of humor and so on, until we have put all the favorable qualities into a mythical man in our mind. Our eyes take in many factors that we believe would make us satisfied. If we are honest, I think the thing that we yearn for the most in our relationships is to simply be loved by a man and to love him back. For the unmarried woman, it can seem as though everyone around her has found a partner that they love in such a way. On the other hand, the married woman may wrongly spend much of her time seeing what her own husband is lacking, while noticing positive characteristics of her friends' husbands. It is a dangerous game to compare our marriages with others' or believe that our future marriage will bring us all we desire relationally. We only see the surface of people's relationships. Every marriage has its strengths and weaknesses, just as every person does. We need to recognize that while we have a good longing to be married, our eyes can lead us to believe that it is worth doing anything or marrying anyone in order to find the relationship of our dreams.

Often, we stop looking at what we want to have relationally and instead focus on what we need to *become* in order to get married. While this may sound like a good thing, it is easy to chase after the wrong traits to emulate. As we look around our world, we see that men admire beautiful women. In our quest to be wanted, we have become a society of women that chase beauty. We see clothes, gym memberships, the new fad diet, a pair of shoes, a new haircut, or some other beauty regimen and believe that if we can just become beautiful, we will become desirable. We also chase success, competence, approval and financial stability to add to our list of appealing attributes. Our eyes allow us to see both what we want to have and what we need to become in order to find relational fulfillment. If we do not check our seeing with the truth of God's Word, then we will quickly begin to covet relationally.

We covet: A Spouse

Our good desire for a relationship can easily turn to coveting when we believe in the promises of marriage over the promises of God. To begin with, we will look at how coveting can emerge in the heart of the unmarried. This group includes women who have never married as well as women who are widowed or divorced. Each of these women experiences different longings. The woman who has never married may wonder if she will ever get to experience the joys of a loving, committed relationship. The widow may struggle with deep longings and loneliness as she misses her spouse. The divorced woman may share the loneliness and longings of the widow, yet may also experience jealousy and feelings of failure as she thinks about her ex-husband. All of these longings, taken to the Lord and entrusted to Him, are normal and not necessarily covetous. However, there are four signs that expose when our longings have become covetous.

First of all, the unmarried woman can know that she is coveting relationally when she finds herself living outside the commands of Scripture. Paul commands those in Corinth to 'flee from sexual immorality. All other sins a man commits are outside his body, but he who sins sexually sins against his own body.'[12] If an unmarried woman is engaging in sexual intimacy outside the covenant of marriage, then her desire for relationship is covetous in nature.

Secondly, if she has set her affections upon a married man, then she is coveting. If you find yourself drawn to a married man at work or in your church, you must quell that desire. It is covetous for you to spend your mental energies thinking about him or attempting to get to know him better. It is not improper to encourage or befriend a married man as our brother in Christ, but it is wrong to have affection for him in a romantic way.

---

12 1 Corinthians 6:18

Another sign that longings have turned covetous is how we relate to friends who are married or engaged. If you cannot rejoice when a friend becomes engaged or attend a friend's wedding, then most likely your own desire for a relationship has taken on a bitter edge. If you are unable to remain close with your married friends simply because they have a spouse, this withdrawal demonstrates a tendency that usually results from coveting. Or, perhaps you remain friends with them, but inwardly have little sympathy for them when their life is difficult because they have a husband, the one thing you desire. The covetous desire for relationship greatly affects our ability to love others.

Lastly, a sure sign of coveting relationally is that we begin to believe that we would be joyful and content if only we could get married. If you find yourself blaming many of your problems on your lack of a husband, it is a sign of a problem in your heart. I think of it as the sighing '*if only*' problem. *If only* I had a husband, I wouldn't have to deal with this housing problem. *If only* I had a husband, I wouldn't have to mow my yard. *If only* I had a husband, I'd have someone to help me with my car. *If only* I had a husband, I'd have someone to enjoy this beautiful sunset with me. We blame our discontentment on our singleness and find ourselves spiraling into a descent of sadness, lacking joy in the good things that God has provided.

Married women can also find themselves coveting relationally. Obviously, sexual intimacy with anyone other than a spouse results from sinful desires. It is also covetous for a married woman to find deep emotional intimacy with any man other than their husband. Again, we can have friendships with men who work with us or know from church, but we must make efforts to remain guarded emotionally in our friendships with them. Our spouse should be our closest confidant and friend. If any other male becomes the one we are sharing our life with on a regular basis, even though the relationship is not physical in nature, it can still be covetous.

Another place married women need to carefully rein in their desires is in comparing their spouse to their friend's spouse. Perhaps one friend's husband is great at planning special date nights. Or another friend's husband prays with her and leads her well spiritually. Another friend's husband earns a large income that can provide nice luxuries for their family. We can begin to focus and think about all the benefits of other husbands and grow numb to all the things we originally loved about our own husband. Married women can also suffer from the sighing *if only* problem. *If only* my husband could fix things, then my life would be so much easier. *If only* my husband could get a better job. *If only* my husband could help me more around the house. *If only* my husband was more engaging with the children. *If only* my husband didn't travel so much. Married women play the same *if only* game and spin a web of discontentment. If we blame our lack of joy on our husband's failings, then it is a sure sign that coveting has grown in our heart.

We covet: Worldly Beauty

As we covet relationally, it is easy to fall into the trap of coveting a particular means of gaining attention from men: beauty. Our inordinate longings for the favor of men can spur on a covetous desire for worldly beauty. In the section on desiring rightly, I will speak to the *true beauty* that we should long for as women. For now, we will explore several characteristics of worldly beauty. First of all, worldly beauty arises from an inordinate desire to be loved. The root of worldly beauty is not to reflect the beauty of the Creator; instead it is focused on self-gain. Secondly, worldly beauty is outward and youthful, fading over time. Thirdly, it speaks 'look at me' and entices men instead of encouraging them. It is a beauty focused on power and control, rather than humility and love. Finally, worldly beauty worships and seeks to exalt self. A covetous longing for beauty will ultimately take on these characteristics and may result in relationships, but most likely not the type that our heart truly desires. As our covetous desires for relationships and beauty grow, we will ultimately take from others.

We take

When we are coveting relationally, we take in a variety of ways. We take joy from friends who are experiencing health in their own relationships by failing to rejoice with them. We take from ways that we could use our singleness for God's glory by selfishly attempting to fill our lives with our own pleasures. We take purity away by dressing in revealing clothing, attempting to attract men by our body instead of our spirit. We take from our husband's reputation by complaining about him and comparing him to others. We take hours that could have been spent growing a relationship with the Lord to chase relationships with men. We take from marriages by flirting with married men and allowing them to have easy emotional connections with us. We take time and energy from our own husband when we expect him to fill all our relational desires. We take and take and take and never feel the fullness that we desire from relationship.

We hide

Our coveting and taking will lead us to hide, even from ourselves. We hide the inappropriate emotional connection under the wrong belief that 'it's not physical, so it's not hurting anyone.' We hide our complaints about our husband as prayer requests. We hide our dissatisfaction with singleness by pursuing pleasure or by priding ourselves on not being that 'desperate girl'. We hide the sinfulness of our inappropriate clothing choices by making the excuse, 'everyone else is wearing it'. We hide because we do not want to feel the pain that can come in our loneliness, nor face the reality that our inward desires might not be satisfied in any earthly relationship. We also do not want to face the fact that some of the consequences we bear are the direct result of our own choices.

We suffer consequences

Just as David faced the consequences of his covetous actions, so will we suffer from walking outside of God's good ways for us relationally. We suffer broken hearts and other emotional scars from building relationships with men we should have avoided. We suffer all sorts of consequences from sexual impropriety: STDs, abortions, feelings of unworthiness, divorce, spiritual dryness and increasing difficulty in fleeing further sexual immorality. We suffer consequences in friendships as bitterness makes us difficult to be around and we lose friends. Our relationship with the Lord may suffer as we distance ourselves from Him because of anger and resentment. In that way, we distance ourselves from the grace that could be ours. It is only as we begin to seek the Lord in our relationships with men that we will be able to find satisfaction in them.

Putting On a New Pattern: Seek the Lord

If we want to find fulfillment in our relationships, then we must begin by developing and growing in our relationship with the Lord. As C.S. Lewis aptly states:

> When I have learnt to love God better than my earthly dearest, I shall love my earthly dearest better than I do now. Insofar as I learn to love my earthly dearest at the expense of God and instead of God, I shall be moving towards the state in which I shall not love my earthly dearest at all. When first things are put first, second things are not suppressed but increased.[13]

If we want to love our husbands well in marriage or long well for a husband during singleness, we must turn our focus to our relationship with the Lord. We should realize from the beginning that if we belong to Christ, we are already part of the truest romance of all of history. Every

13 C.S. Lewis, *The Collected Letters of C.S. Lewis*, Volume III (New York: HarperCollins, 2007).

other romance that has ever been experienced or written about is just a shadow of the greater and grander love story of Christ and His church. The book of Revelation, and all of earth's history, ends with a wedding. All of the beauty and joy that accompanies our earthly weddings will truly find fullness and satisfaction at *that* wedding. Those in the church are Christ's Bride, waiting for the day when we will hear, 'Let us rejoice and be glad and give him glory! For the wedding of the Lamb has come, and his bride has made herself ready. Fine linen, bright and clean, was given her to wear.'[14] As we seek the Lord with our earthly relational desires, we first need to believe two important truths about Christ's relationship with His church.

The first truth concerns God's active pursuit of us. All of the Scriptures speak to God's creating and pursuing a people to love and cherish. However, I want to take a moment to look at one specific exchange that contrasts our earthy desire for relationship with our relationship with God. In his Gospel, John records the story of Jesus speaking with a Samaritan woman that He met while He was sitting at a well. She came to draw water, and Jesus engaged in conversation with her. This fact alone surprised her because she was a Samaritan and Jews did not associate with them. She was all the more surprised when He told her, 'Everyone who drinks this water will be thirsty again, but whoever drinks the water I give him will never thirst. Indeed, the water I give him will become in him a spring of water welling up to eternal life.'[15] To this she replied, 'Sir, give me this water.'[16] Jesus then asked her to go and call her husband. When she replied that she had no husband, Jesus affirmed that she was correct and said, 'The fact is, you have had five husbands, and the man you

---

14 Revelation 19:7-8

15 John 4:13-14

16 John 4:15

now have is not your husband. What you have just said is quite true.'[17] His statement gives the reader a window into the relational struggles of this woman. She may have been widowed or divorced multiple times and now was living with a man to whom she was not married. Certainly her life had experienced deep brokenness and pain. Just as she came back time and time again to that well for water and never found true satisfaction, she had gone through relationship after relationship with men and never found contentment.

However, once she meets with Jesus, everything in her life changes. She leaves her water jug and goes back into town, telling others about Jesus. She who had been empty now became a 'spring of water welling up to eternal life.' In fact, many of the Samaritans in that town believed in Jesus because of her testimony. It was her relationship with Jesus that breathed life into all of her other relationships. Jesus pursued her and spoke with her even though she was a woman, a Samaritan and living with a man who was not her husband. If we want to find contentment, we must believe that Christ's pursuit of us and our relationship with Him is the wellspring of all our other relationships. We should also take hope that no one is too sinful for His pursuit or too broken to be healed by His love.

The second truth we need to believe is that we have been loved with the greatest love imaginable. Jesus told His disciples, 'Greater love has no one than this, that he lay down his life for his friends.'[18] If you are a Christian – single, married, widowed or divorced – you must realize that the most significant love affair of your life began when you believed in Christ. Our covetous desires for relationship show that our heart has grown cold to our first love. The angel speaking to the church in Ephesus warned, 'You have forsaken your first love. Remember the height from which

17 John 4:18

18 John 15:13

you have fallen! Repent and do the things you did at first.'[19] The first thing we did when we came to Christ was to *believe* in Him. We fan the flame of our belief in Christ by living in daily relationship with Him. We come to Him, drinking from the fount of living water, that we might have life in all our other relationships. If we seek to gain from others what we should only gain from Christ, we will experience failure and frustration in our marital and dating relationships.

Let me also say that while we find our greatest love and acceptance in Jesus, this fact does not always change the painful circumstances we face in our marriages or singleness. Women who love Jesus dearly still experience the pain of divorce, adultery, loss and loneliness. However, Psalm 68 rejoices, 'A father to the fatherless, a defender of widows, is God in his holy dwelling. God sets the lonely in families.'[20] If you are lonely, pray that God would set you in a family to give you love, support and companionship. If you are in a family, seek to include those who may be lonely into your family. As we grow in our love for the Lord, the difficult circumstances we may face are comforted by His greater love for us. The painful brokenness of unstable earthly relationships will not overwhelm us because we have one relationship that nothing can divide. As Paul writes, 'For I am convinced that neither death nor life, neither angels nor demons, neither the present nor the future, nor any powers, neither height nor depth, nor anything else in all creation, will be able to separate us from the love of God that is in Christ Jesus our Lord.'[21] No earthly relationship can give such promise. Instead, we must remember the depth of His love for us by spending time knowing Him through His Word and taking our desires to Him in prayer.

---

19 Revelation 2:4-5

20 Psalm 68:5-6

21 Romans 8:38-39

Desire rightly

If we want to fight our tendency to covet a romantic relationship, we must begin to desire rightly. Doing so begins with a greater desire to know the Lord and be in an ever-increasing relationship with Him. From that initial desire, we will develop a right desire for beauty. This process involves growing in desire for *true beauty* and putting off our desires for worldly beauty. Below, we will contrast these two types of beauty and observe what the Bible teaches about how to develop into a beautiful woman.

First of all, Proverbs states, 'Charm is deceptive, and beauty is fleeting; but a woman who fears the Lord is to be praised.'[22] While worldly beauty begins with an inordinate desire to be loved, true beauty begins with a fear of the Lord. Heartfelt respect for the Lord brings lasting admiration, while outward charm and beauty fail to endure the seasons of life.

Secondly, worldly beauty is outward, youthful and fading, while true beauty is inward and unfading. Peter tells women, 'Your beauty should not come from outward adornment such as braided hair and the wearing of gold jewelry and fine clothes. Instead it should be that of your inner self, the unfading beauty of a gentle and quiet spirit, which is of great worth in God's sight.'[23] My friend Connice exemplifies this verse to me. She has lovely clothes, often wears cute jewelry and knows how to put an outfit together well. However, her beauty does not come from what she wears on the outside. Instead, she reflects Christ's love through the warmth of her smile and her gentleness towards others. As she shares godly wisdom, she radiates unfading beauty.

This type of beauty often shines the most once our outward youthfulness has passed. I met a woman last year who was in her early seventies (although I think she only

22 Proverbs 31:30

23 1 Peter 3:3-4

admitted to sixty-nine). As she shared with me some stories about her life, I was amazed to hear about the struggles and difficulties she had suffered. The trials of her circumstances did not match the joy and beauty that radiated from her gentle and quiet spirit. Far from being weighed down by the burdens of life, she seemed to soar in her spirit. Hers was a beauty that shone and could not be contained by skin that might wrinkle or hair that might grey. While worldly beauty requires surgery and creams that will ultimately fail to preserve youth, she exhibited the unfading beauty that flowed from her deep love for the Lord.

Thirdly, while worldly beauty entices, 'Come to me', true beauty encourages, 'Come to Jesus.' Paul speaks to this when he reminds the Romans, 'How beautiful are the feet of those who bring good news.'[24] Rather than desire that others would be attracted to us, we should desire that our life and actions attract them to Jesus. Our hope should be that we live in such a way that shines forth His love and goodness and that our words speak the gospel to those around us. Short skirts and low cut tops may entice men, but true beauty encourages them to know the Lord.

Lastly, worldly beauty worships self, while true beauty worships Jesus. When Mary came to Jesus to prepare Him for His burial, she poured expensive perfume on His head and wiped His feet with her hair. Jesus silenced the disciples' harsh rebuke of her by saying, 'Why are you bothering this woman? She has done a beautiful thing to me.'[25] Here, in this story, we have a picture of beauty: a woman bringing all she has and bowing down in humility to worship Jesus. She faced rebuke and embarrassment, but her love and affection for Him was greater than her fear of others' opinions. If we want to be beautiful, we start by worshipping the Lord. When that becomes our desire, beauty will follow.

24 Romans 10:15

25 Matthew 26:10

GIVE GENEROUSLY

As we seek the Lord and desire rightly in our relationships, we will begin to become women who give generously. A covetous woman seeks her own gain in her relationships with men. However, a woman who is filled with the love of the Lord can give to others. She can encourage marriages in her church and rejoice when they flourish. She can give forgiveness to a spouse who has wronged her because she knows how much she has been forgiven. She can choose to speak well of her ex-husband to her children, even though he may speak unkind words about her. She can seek to encourage men as brothers in the faith, rather than enticing them with her flirtations. She serves her husband in love and does not catalogue his faults to herself or others. Most of all, she gives great glory and honor to God, full of thankfulness in her relationship with Him.

CONFESS FREELY

We will all have seasons of difficulty in our desire for the love and affection of a spouse. Whether we are single or married, we may find ourselves overcome with loneliness and hopelessness. The single woman may believe that life is passing her by as she spends her days alone. The married woman may feel that being alone would be better than the emotional isolation she feels from her spouse. Or, desire may grow towards someone outside of God's plan for us. The single or married woman may find herself attracted to someone already married. If you are feeling overwhelmed by loneliness or by sinful desires towards someone who is not your spouse, find a friend you trust to share your struggle with you. Confess, knowing that you are not alone in your struggle. James gives us hope that, 'The prayer of a righteous man is powerful and effective.'[26]

I want to close this chapter with two stories from friends of mine who have struggled with inordinate or culpable

---

26 James 5:16

relational desires. Their names have been changed so that they could freely share their stories in their own words. If, after reading their accounts, you see yourself in them, take the time to find help. Confession is the first step on the path towards healing.

Story of Sarah, a single friend

I became a Christian early in my college years, and with my faith came a deep conviction about physical relationships with men. From my high school dating experience, I knew the great temptation that comes with even the smallest bit of intimacy, so I avoided this sin diligently. As I reached my mid-twenties still single, I began to doubt the importance of physical purity. Was it really so important? In retrospect, I've realized that this doubt rose from a much bigger doubt, that God's promises are really true, and that His plans are for our good.

I got into a serious dating relationship that quickly became very physical. I knew that I wasn't supposed to have sex, but everything in me wanted to. I thought I had waited long enough, so we began having sex. Sex outside of marriage proved to be physically and emotionally exhilarating. I did not think I would marry him, but I loved the intimacy of our relationship.

We broke up, and soon I found myself dating and having sex with another guy. Sex once again was a physical and emotional thrill for me. About two weeks after he and I started having sex, I knew something was very wrong with me. After much physical pain, emotional distress and countless tears, my doctor diagnosed me with herpes, one of the few STDs that is incurable. I've never felt so dirty, and so unlovable.

As you can imagine, this diagnosis hit me really hard. The challenge wasn't just getting diagnosed with an STD, but facing the reality of the choices I'd made over the past year. I'd sinned in a way that hurt my body, but even more, in a way that hurt my soul. My relationship with God has suffered tremendously. I still struggle with doubting that His laws are for our good and for our protection, even though I've seen firsthand what consequences come with breaking His laws. Though I know the theology of grace, I feel as though grace is not available to me. I'm incredibly ashamed that I have an STD, and have a tremendous fear of dating any godly guy, for fear he will reject me because of my past actions. I've also had a hard time getting out of a sexual relationship with the guy I got herpes from. I know it sounds crazy, but he knows my ugliest secret, so I don't fear rejection with him. I also have tasted the pleasure of sex, and have found it hard to turn down this pleasure when the opportunity comes up.

Where is the redemption in this story? I am still waiting, struggling with brokenness, guilt, shame and an appetite for sin. I know I am missing the joy I had before all of this, a joy I want to have again, but it just feels so far away. I guess one piece of the redemption is the grace that has been demonstrated to me in this whole process through the work of an extremely compassionate doctor who has gone far beyond her duties to care for me as a patient. God has also provided friends (new and old) who, despite my outward and inward rebellion, have loved me and spoken truth to me. Still, I hope that there is more to come.

Story of Margaret, a married friend

I never thought I would struggle with relational desires outside of my marriage. I'm much too much of a 'rule follower' for that! So how did I slowly find myself enticed by a man other than my husband? The Bible says that it happens like this, 'but each one is tempted when, by (her) own evil desire, (she) is dragged away and enticed. Then, after desire has conceived, it gives birth to sin; and sin, when it is full-grown, gives birth to death' (James 1:14-15).

For me, it happened exactly like that. My own evil desire manifested in wanting a husband who fulfilled specific requirements I thought necessary, instead of being content and thankful for the one God gave me. Helping clean up after dinner, putting the kids to bed, taking the trash out, loving me well. While not wrong in and of themselves, those desires quickly became sinful when I saw another man fulfilling them better than my husband. His offering to clean up after dinner, playing with the kids and showing gratitude for a nice meal all looked very nice. So began a growing discontentment in my own marriage. Each day brought another tick in the negative column for my husband, while each encounter with the other man brought another checkmark in his positive column. I was getting dragged away and enticed for sure. I found myself thinking more and more about what my life would be like with him. What if something happened to my own husband? Maybe that wouldn't be so bad. Whoa! Did that really cross my mind? Now, I've jumped from the seventh commandment to the sixth! Those desires were being conceived and giving birth to sin. And that sin would grow and give birth to death. These emotions had to be dealt with, and swiftly!

Although I quickly identified the problem and tried to repent, it wasn't as easy I thought it should be. While I did not act on my feelings, they were present nonetheless. It seemed that no matter how hard I tried not to think about him, I still did. I had given the devil a foothold he would not quickly give up. I went along for several months in this way, just trying harder to forget about him. Unfortunately, this would not be a sin without consequences.

So how did I get out of it? I had already confessed to the Lord and asked for forgiveness, but now I felt a strong need to confess this sin openly. But to whom? Since it dealt with my husband, I decided I needed to tell him. That was a difficult conversation indeed! God was gracious in that encounter and has continued to show me His love through my husband. He forgave me and chose to enter into my struggle rather than running away. I have seen firsthand that 'Though one may be overpowered, two can defend themselves. A cord of three strands is not quickly broken' (Eccles. 4:12).

What I have learned is that I am actually an adulterer at heart. I am unfaithful to the core. My unfaithfulness comes from a lack of contentment in what God has given me. And it will remain unless God changes me and gives me a heart of gratitude and complete trust in Him, who has given me all things I need to be made into His likeness.

Conclusion: God's grace is sufficient

From these examples, I hope you see the depth of pain that can result when our relational desires become covetous. I also hope you remember that the grace of Christ is sufficient to rescue each of us both from the penalty and the power of these lusts in our lives. As we confess to one another, prayerfully seeking the Lord in all our relationships, we will begin to love others in a way that is honoring and encouraging. We will continue to observe this deep longing for relationships in the next chapter as we see the effect that our desires can have on our relationships with friends and family members.

Questions for Personal Reflection and Group Discussion

1. How can you observe the desire for romantic relationships in the world today? What are signs in our society that often these desires have become inordinate or culpable?
2. Read 2 Samuel 11–12:14. How do you see the progression of 'see, covet, take and hide' in this passage?

3. What consequences does David suffer? How does God also show him mercy?
4. David had spent years in adversity, being chased and threatened by Saul. Yet, his moment of greatest sin came in prosperity. How can prosperity often be a place of great temptation?
5. How do both single women and married women covet romantic relationships? How do we compare and complain in our own situation? How is each person tempted to play the '*if only*' game?
6. Read 1 Corinthians 6:18. Why is sexual immorality particularly precarious? What ways do we see suffering result from sexual immorality?
7. How do we covet beauty? What are specific ways women today pursue beauty at any cost? How does this desire for worldly beauty seep into the church?
8. Read Proverbs 31:30, 1 Peter 3:3-4, Romans 10:15, and Matthew 26:10. How does the Biblical depiction of beauty differ from a worldly picture of beauty?
9. How does coveting romantic relationships and beauty cause us to take from those around us? How do we hide our selfish desires?
10. Read John 4:7-28, 39. How do we know this woman had experienced the painful brokenness of relationships in her life? How did her relationship with Jesus change her life and her relationships? How has your relationship with Jesus changed your relationships?
11. Read Romans 8:38-39. Why is our relationship with Jesus our only certain relationship? What are ways we can cultivate and grow that relationship?

7 Coveting within Family and Friendship

There can be no doubt that this possessive clinging to things is one of the most harmful habits in the life. Because it is so natural it is rarely recognized for the evil that it is; but its outworkings are tragic. We are often hindered from giving up our treasures to the Lord out of fear for their safety; this is especially true when those treasures are loved relatives and friends. But we need have no such fears. Our Lord came not to destroy but to save. Everything is safe which we commit to Him, and nothing is really safe which is not so committed.

A.W. Tozer

The Pursuit of God
(Camp Hill: Christian Publications,1982), pp. 27-8

7

Coveting within Family and Friendship:

The Story of Joseph

As I look back over friendships throughout my childhood years, I can remember distinctly the ways we defined friendship. We made friendship bracelets or pins and gave them to each other. We designed secret notebooks, decorated on the front with magazine cutouts, and used them to write notes to one another during class. We established neighborhood clubs and spent hours in the woods thinking up names and building forts. When one friend became particularly close, we would declare ourselves 'BFF' and seal our commitment to one another with broken heart necklaces. One half of the heart belonged to each best friend, with her name engraved on your half and your name engraved on her half. Each girl wore her necklace while experiencing the joy of both having and being a best friend. As I think back to all of our childhood outward demonstrations of affection, it seems evident that they simply displayed our inner desire to belong. Even at a young age, we are aware that we need others in our lives. It is also apparent that it is easy for that longing to become covetous.

When I was in elementary school, I had a good friend named Martha. She lived just down the road, and often we would play together in the afternoons. At some point, I found out she had another friend named Karla from a different neighborhood whom she considered her 'best friend'. The knowledge that Karla was her closest friend immediately left a sour taste in my mouth. I became convinced that Karla didn't like me, and I was pretty certain that I didn't really like Karla. Notwithstanding the fact that I barely knew Karla, my own desire to be Martha's best friend led me to be both distrustful of Karla and recoil at the idea of building a friendship with her.

These covetous patterns can easily follow us into the teen years and throughout our friendships with women and our families. One of my dear friends, Tracy, came from a difficult family situation that always left her longing for a mother figure in her life. After the tragic death of her father, the need was even more pronounced. The Lord faithfully provided her with a mentor named Susan to walk through life with her and provide spiritual mothering along the way. However, early in their relationship, Tracy found herself becoming increasingly jealous when Susan would mentor other women. In the back of her mind certain questions lingered: 'Does she have enough love to go around?' 'Is she going to forget about me?' At times, it was difficult to be friends with these other women because she was fearful of losing the motherly love she desired from Susan. Rather than trusting in the Lord's provision, she began to cling to the relationship.

In this chapter, we are going to transition from the desire for romantic affection to exploring our desire for relationship as it relates to our friendships and families. These potentially covetous desires present themselves in a variety of ways. Some women experience painful unmet longings within their own families. If these desires are not met in an ever-deepening relationship with Christ, then over time discontent and bitterness will encrust her heart, leading to more brokenness in her familial relationships. Others play the comparison game in friendships, always attempting to find significance and be significant in the lives of others. This incorrect source of identity leads them to feel threatened when their friends develop new friendships or make choices different than their own.

If we want to escape these relational dramas, we need to realize that true freedom and health can begin in our relationships as we grow in our relationship with the Lord. My friend Tracy eventually experienced freedom in such a way with Susan that she has been able to encourage Susan to invest in the lives of other women. The irony of my elementary school story involving Martha and Karla is that eventually, in middle school, Martha moved away. Karla and I got to know each other and by high school were leading a Bible study together every week at her home. We attended college together and went on to be bridesmaids in each other's weddings. Had I continued in my earlier insecurities, I would have missed the enjoyment of many years of friendship.

In order to study this type of relational coveting, we will turn back to Genesis and study the family of Joseph. His story demonstrates the brokenness that can result from generations of coveting and envy being passed down within a family. We will also look at the particular ways we as women sometimes put unfair relational expectations on our friends and families. Our covetous desires in this area begin when we wrongly seek for our needs to be met in these relationships rather than growing in our walk with Christ. Ultimately, this possessiveness brings unfavorable consequences that can spiral us deeper into relational coveting. To conclude this chapter, we will once again look at what truths about God we need to understand in order to fight this pattern in our lives. Growth in our relationship with the Lord will ultimately lead to freedom in our relationships with others.

Joseph's story starts in detail in the thirty-seventh chapter of Genesis. However, his story (like all of our stories) actually begins during the generations just before him. Joseph was the son of Jacob and Rachel, and the grandson of Isaac and Rebekah. While she was pregnant with twins, Rebekah felt within her womb the rivalry that would eventually lead to deception and disunity in her family. As the children grew, we are told that 'Isaac, who had a taste for wild game, loved Esau, but Rebekah loved Jacob.'[1] Parental favoritism led to rivalry between the sons, and eventually Jacob robbed Esau of both his birthright and his blessing. In return, Esau's envy of Jacob's situation led him to plot to kill his own brother.

To protect her favorite son from Esau's murderous revenge, Rebekah sends Jacob to her brother Laban. While Jacob lives with his uncle, he falls in love with Laban's daughter, Rachel. He promises to work seven years in order to be able to marry her. Once the seven years concludes, Laban tricks Jacob and gives him his other daughter Leah to marry instead of Rachel. Jacob, whose name actually means, 'one who deceives', is faced with the harsh reality of being deceived himself. In anger, he confronts Laban, who then promises to also give Rachel to Jacob in exchange for seven more years of labor.

Take a moment to imagine the depth of relational discord that would result from Jacob having two wives. Leah, unloved and miserable, seeks to win her husband's favor by bearing him sons. On the other hand, Rachel, while loved dearly by her husband, remains barren. Genesis 30:1 tells us, 'When Rachel saw that she was not bearing Jacob any children, she became jealous of her sister.' Each woman wants what the other has and becomes locked in a covetous battle to gain the object of her desire. As the story continues, each uses her maidservants to grow the family, and at one point

---

1 Genesis 25:28

Rachel sells an evening with her husband to her sister in order to gain mandrake plants (thought to be an aphrodisiac promoting fertility).[2] Their story is a messy situation that spirals into ever greater pain, discord and envy.

Out of this sisterly rivalry, Joseph is finally born to Rachel. After years of waiting, God remembered Rachel and opened her womb. At this point in the story, it would be easy to speculate and believe that Rachel has it all. Now she has both her husband's love and a son – surely she is content. However, we find a clue to the state of her heart by what she names her son. The name Joseph literally means, 'may he add.' Rachel's prayer as she names him is, 'May the Lord add to me another son.' Rather than enjoying what she has been given, Rachel is already asking for more. In many ways, the simple cry of the covetous could be summed up in the phrase, 'may he add.' Once again, we see that getting what we want does not lead to the contentment we desire. It is too easy to look over the fence at our neighbor and to ignore our own treasures as soon as we see another's blessings. While Rachel was blessed with a son, her sister Leah had just given birth to her sixth son. Rachel was not satisfied with simply having a child; her desires and longing were based on her rivalry with her sister. Their relational envy would continue and eventually pass to the next generation, affecting each of their sons.

It is into this generational quagmire that Joseph is born and grows into manhood. By the time we hear more of his situation, he is a young man of seventeen, tending the flocks with his brothers. The story tells us that Joseph brought his father a bad report about his brothers. From what occurs later in the story, we can safely assume that Joseph was not exaggerating in his report. We are also told that Jacob loved Joseph more than any of his brothers and

---

2 *Spirit of the Reformation Study Bible*, (Grand Rapids: Zondervan, 2003) notes on Genesis 30:14; 62.

made Joseph a richly ornamented robe. It is from this point, that we can witness the covetous pattern work itself out among the brothers.

They Saw

Genesis 37:4 tells us, 'When his brothers saw that their father loved [Joseph] more than any of them, they hated him and could not speak a kind word to him.'[3] The richly ornamented robe was simply an outward sign to each of the brothers of their father's affection. The situation only got worse when Joseph began relating his dreams to them. Joseph's dreams foretold that his own brothers, and even his parents, would bow down to him. While they were already forced to observe their father's affection, now they were given a vision of their younger brother's preeminence over each of them. What they saw quickly led them to jealousy of their younger brother's situation.

They Coveted

Joseph's brothers were faced with a true injustice. They had a right longing for their father's affection and love. Jacob followed the pattern set by his own parents and harmed all of his sons by choosing to favor one of them. While Jacob was not right in his actions, his sons failed to trust God with the injustice they faced. Instead, their hearts became darkened with ever-increasing hatred and jealousy.[4] They were so embittered that they could not even speak kindly to Joseph. However, their unkind words were just the tip of the iceberg of the ways these brothers would take from Joseph.

They Took

One day, Jacob sent Joseph to go and check on his brothers as they were tending their flocks. When the brothers saw

---

3 Genesis 37:4

4 Genesis 37:8, 11

Joseph coming from a distance, they planned to murder him and put a stop to all his dreams. Reuben, the oldest brother, interceded and convinced his brothers not to shed Joseph's blood. Instead, the brothers stripped him of his robe and threw him into a dry cistern. Ignoring Joseph's cries, the brothers callously sat down to eat their meal. While they were eating, a caravan of Ishmaelites traveled by on their way to Egypt. Judah convinced his brothers that it would be much better to sell their brother into slavery than to kill him as they had planned. In order to satisfy their hatred and anger, they sold their brother for twenty shekels of silver. Their covetous desires drove them to rob Joseph of his robe, his family, and his inheritance. They also brought great suffering to their father, Jacob, and essentially proved the selfishness of their love for him. They craved his love and affection, yet they must have known the pain it would cause their father to lose his beloved son. Therefore, they chose to hide what they had done.

They Hid

The brothers attempted to hide their sin against Joseph by taking his ornamented robe and dipping it in the blood of a slaughtered goat. They took it back to their father, claiming to have found it as they journeyed home. Jacob, the deceiver, is once again deceived. He believes a ferocious animal devoured Joseph, tearing him to pieces. Bereft of his beloved son, Jacob tears his clothes, puts on sackcloth, refuses comfort from any of his children and claims, 'in mourning will I go to the grave to my son.'[5] The brothers could hide their sin from their father, but they could not escape the reality of their father's love and affection for Joseph. Even in death, their covetous desires were not satisfied, as the love given to Joseph in life was replaced by mourning over his death.

---

5 Genesis 37:35

They Bore Consequences

It is important to note that none of the brothers got what they wanted. None of them became the new favored child (and perhaps none of them truly wanted this role after seeing what happened to Joseph). Instead, they had to live each day with the consequences of their actions. As they daily faced Jacob's suffering, they dealt with the reality of their own choices. They came to believe that they deserved any and every suffering that came upon them. Years later, there was a terrible famine and the only place to buy grain was in Egypt. When the brothers arrived in Egypt and attempted to purchase food, the governor of the land accused them of being spies. Their response speaks volumes about the guilt that they have lived with for all of these years, for they say to one another, 'Surely we are being punished because of our brother. We saw how distressed he was when he pleaded with us for his life, but we would not listen; that's why this distress has come upon us.'[6]

Unbeknownst to each of them, the governor is actually their own brother, Joseph. He hears their conversation and weeps. Although Joseph has risen to great heights in Egypt, he has suffered deeply throughout the years since his brothers sold him into slavery. At this point, he is in the exact same position that his brothers were in so many years earlier. Just as his brothers suffered the injustice of their father's favoritism, Joseph suffered great injustice because of his brother's actions. At this point, Joseph has the power to repay his brothers for all the evil that they have done to him.

THEY EXPERIENCE GRACE

Instead, Joseph walks in the way of Christ by his response. Rather than taking justice into his own hands, he 'entrusted himself to him who judges justly.'[7] Joseph's belief in God

---

6 Genesis 42:21

7 1 Peter 2:23

allowed him to not only forgive his brothers, but to do good to them in every way. Eventually, all of his family came to live with him in Egypt, and he provided them with everything they needed to survive the famine. Joseph's years of wandering and injustice had not caused bitterness to harden his heart. Instead, he had grown in grace and understanding of God's ways. After Jacob died, Joseph's brothers came to him, throwing themselves down and saying, 'We are your slaves.' Joseph's response was simply amazing and full of mercy. '... He [Joseph] said to them, "Don't be afraid. Am I in the place of God? You intended to harm me, but God intended it for good to accomplish what is now being done, the saving of many lives. So then, don't be afraid. I will provide for you and your children." And he reassured them and spoke kindly to them.'[8] The brothers, whose covetous hatred prevented them from saying a kind word to Joseph, were met with kind words and reassurance. If the brothers are an example of the painful consequences of relational coveting, Joseph exemplifies the bountiful fruit of belief and trust in God.

The relational envy that flowed throughout the generations of Abraham's offspring may appear within our own families and friendships. Discord abounds, and many families and churches are marked more by petty squabbles than grace and peace. As our eyes become fixated on our own desires in relationships, we fall into the same covetous pattern as Joseph's brothers.

We See

Many of us have an image of what we believe our lives should look like relationally. It may involve the family happily sitting around a board game, enjoying time together. It may be dinner out with a group of girlfriends, staying up late enjoying meaningful conversation. It may be holding a baby of one's own and experiencing the joys of motherhood. It may involve

8 Genesis 50:19-21

co-workers that are easy to get along with and a boss who notices diligence and rewards it accordingly. We can quite easily dream up perfection in our minds. When our reality does not live up to the vision in our mind, we may become dissatisfied relationally. Slowly, we begin to observe other people's relationships and believe they are experiencing full life, while our own relationships are mired in frustration.

Many women are a bit of an Anne Shirley, waiting and longing for a kindred spirit to come into her life and fill her relationally. In the book, *Anne of Green Gables*, Anne shared her dream of friendship to the ever-realistic and practical Marilla, describing, 'A bosom friend – an intimate friend, you know – a really kindred spirit to whom I can confide my inmost soul. I've dreamed of meeting her all of my life.'[9] We long to have someone to share our hopes, dreams, fears and struggles.

While it is good to desire deep and intimate relationships with other women, at times we can become particularly distrustful as we observe relationships around us. If one notices two friends out to lunch, she may come to the conclusion that those friends must not like her, simply because they failed to ask her along. If two moms meet at the park with their children, another mom might wonder if her own children are difficult to be around and that is why no one asked her to come along. Another woman watches as a group of co-workers plan to have dinner after work and sits wondering quietly to herself why no one asked her to come along. New mediums of relating, such as Facebook, allow people to quietly observe other people's friendships. As we examine others' relationships in a variety of ways, we have the tendency to become increasingly discontent in our own.

At other times, we can also observe what we simply may not have relationally. When I lived overseas, I gave birth to my first little girl. I would see other moms spending time

9 L.M. Montgomery, *Anne of Green Gables* (New York: HarperCollins, 1908) pp. 73-4.

with their own mothers, and feel the desire of wanting my own mom nearby. It was easy to believe that having my own mom close at hand would make all the transitions of motherhood easier to manage. For others, it might be that a mother or mother-in-law is nearby, but there remains distance in the relationship because of past hurts and discord. While it is good to long for deep, intimate relationships, these desires can become idolatrous in nature if our observation of others leads us to discontentment and bitterness. These feelings are sure signs that our seeing and longing has turned to coveting.

We Covet

As we linger and consider our relational desires, we can choose to hope in the Lord to fulfill those longings, or we can find ourselves growing increasingly discontent and disgruntled within the relationships closest to us. We complain that our church fails to care for our particular needs well. We compare the help we receive from extended family to our neighbor, whose family and in-laws live in town and are always available to help. We compare the amount of time that one friend spends with another, concerned about being left out. We hear of a kindness shown from one friend to another, and rather than rejoice, we quietly lament, 'Why can't I have friends who love me like that?' We grow suspicious when others make choices different than our own because we secretly wonder if we might be left friendless by choosing a different path. The comparison game played in friendship is at best naïve, in that we cannot truly know the depth of someone else's friendships, and at worst completely self-focused. The covetous woman goes into relationships always hoping to gain from the other person. She is looking for that companion to share her life, but no friend or family member can ever fulfill what her soul is truly longing to encounter. As time passes, she will either become isolated from others as they fail to satisfy her needs, or she will smother and exhaust others in her attempt to cling to their friendship.

We Take

Ultimately, our covetous desire for relationship will lead us to take from those around us. While we take in a variety of ways, I want us to focus on a few specific areas women tend to take relationally. A covetous heart will cause a woman to sin against other women by her words, her use of time and her lack of ministry towards others in friendship. Rather than knowing the joy of healthy friendships, she will experience painful frustration as she relates to others, often blind to her own participation in the demise of her friendships. Instead of keeping friendships for the long haul, these types of takers wear out friendships similarly to the way a little boy wears out the knees in his pant legs. The fabric of the relationship simply cannot withstand the constant wear of a covetous friend.

The primary way we as women take from one another relationally is with our words. We actively sin against each other by what we choose to say, while we passively take from each other by what we fail to say. Usually, it is a jealous, hurting woman who speaks unkind words about another woman. A heart that is embittered relationally will quickly find fault with others. I have watched sadly as one woman is being praised for her character or service, and another women steps in to share some piece of gossip about her in order to tear down her image. The gossiping woman simply cannot sit by and let another woman be praised. She fears honor and respect being given to anyone other than herself. Gossip can also form a false sense of intimacy between two women. As they come together and agree in their dislike or disdain for another person, a bond forms between them. However, the temporary unity experienced often turns to distrust as each wonders, 'If she said that about Jane behind her back, then what does she really think about me?'

It is not only our active words that can harm, but also what we fail to say that can take from others in friendship. Our covetous relational desires cause us to focus on the failures in our friendships instead of being thankful for the ways those around us support and love us. It is easy to focus on the love given to others by their friends, while being blind to the ways the Lord uses our own friends to care for us. Perhaps a friend shares something that really encourages us, but we fail to take the time to thank her because of our continual self-focus. Many times our lack of encouragement and support shows forth the fruit of our inner discontent.

Secondly, we take from friendship by our use of time and our recommendations to friends about how they use their time. It is tempting in friendship to want to cling tightly to relationships that we have enjoyed for years. However, if we selfishly keep only old friends, then we will fail to love those who are new in our churches. I regularly hear from new women in our congregation that while people are outwardly friendly at church, they are relationally closed off. It is not that they are in any way unkind, but they do not allow time for new friendships because they focus all of their attention on established relationships. It requires trust and openness to encourage our friends to build strong relationships with new people. We take time away from building new friendships when we always choose the relationships that are comfortable and satisfy our own needs.

Finally, we take from friendships by failing to minister well within them. We may rob others of a listening ear because our self-focus causes us to talk on and on about ourselves. Or, if we do listen, we fail to speak truth to them because we are afraid of losing their friendship. It takes a relationally content person to be willing to confront a friend who is caught in a sinful pattern. We also take from others by saying that we will pray for them, yet we fail to discipline ourselves to truly minister to them in such an unseen, unselfish way.

The relationally covetous simply approach their friendships wondering, 'What can I get out this friendship?' or perhaps they ask, 'Why haven't my friends noticed my struggle?' instead of thinking, 'How can I serve my friend in love?' They are unable to minister well because they are focused on having their own needs met.

We Hide

Just as Joseph's brothers attempted to hide the effects of their covetous actions, so we try to hide the ways we harm others. We hide our gossip by saying, 'Well, she shared it with everyone at lunch, so I'm sure she wouldn't mind if I told you.' We hide our lack of praise or encouragement by thinking, 'I'm sure she knows how many people have been blessed by her service.' We hide the use of our time by claiming that busyness is what keeps us from welcoming new friendships, when it is truthfully just our own desires to cling to what is comfortable. We hide our failure to minister faithfully in friendships by passing the responsibility to others. We believe that someone else should bring a meal, confront a sin pattern or be that listening ear. In all these ways, we hide from our responsibility to love freely and care well for those whom the Lord has placed in our lives.

If we want to live freely from this negative relational pattern, we need to accept two realities in our relationships with others. First of all, we were created to desire and need intimacy. It is good for us to want and pursue positive relationships in our lives. Secondly, all of our relationships here will be tainted by the effects of Adam's fall in the Garden. None of these relationships can ultimately satisfy us. Our friends and family will all fail to love us perfectly. In the same way, we will fail our family and friends. None of us can satisfy the deep relational needs that each of us experience as we live in a fallen world. If we desire strong friendships and family bonds, then we must once again turn to Christ by believing the gospel and entering into our relationships in new ways.

Seek the Lord

As we seek to escape this type of relational coveting and the negative way it impacts our friendships, we must begin by seeking the Lord in new ways. We must fully accept that our earthly relationships will never fully satisfy because we were created for more. Even if we find our best friend, have loving parents, hold a much-longed-for baby in our arms, or gain wisdom from a mentor, we will still find ourselves longing relationally. Adam and Eve were created for relationship with one another, but they were most importantly created for relationship with the One who formed them. In their sin, they rebelled against that relationship, and all of our relationships suffer the effects. However, the Fall did not diminish our need for our relationship with our Creator; it simply made that relationship impossible without the blood of Christ.

As we seek the Lord relationally, we need to impress upon our hearts the truth of Jeremiah 31:3: 'I have loved you with an everlasting love; I have drawn you with loving-kindness.' All of Scripture speaks to God's loving pursuit of His people in spite of their sin. Our seeking of Him begins because He has first sought each of us. He has drawn us into relationship, pursued us with His love and has promised to be with us wherever we go. The culmination of this desire is met at the cross, where reconciliation was fully, once and for all, purchased for our salvation. The book of Romans speaks to this pursuit by explaining, 'You see, at just the right time, when we were still powerless, Christ died for the ungodly. Very rarely will anyone die for a righteous man, though for a good man someone might possibly dare to die. But God demonstrates his own love for us in this: While we were still sinners, Christ died for us.'[10] Through Christ, God pursued

10 Romans 5:6-8

a relationship with His people, and it is because of that reconciliation that we can experience healing and peace in our relationships with others.

The thought of God's love for us can sustain and encourage us when other relationships fail. David cried out to God, 'My heart says of you, "Seek his face!" Your face, LORD, I will seek. Do not hide your face from me, do not turn your servant away in anger; you have been my helper. Do not reject me or forsake me, O God my Savior. Though my father and mother forsake me, the LORD will receive me.'[11] He speaks to the fact that even the most intimate of relationships, the parent to the child, may fail. Yet, in seeking the Lord, he finds full acceptance and the confidence to hope: 'I will see the goodness of the Lord in the land of the living.'[12] Our relational satisfaction begins when we seek the Lord and entrust all our other relationships to Him. The psalmist describes God as a 'father to the fatherless.'[13] The promise of the Lord's presence gives strength to His people when they are lonely, rejected or separated from those they love. The Christian's greatest strength and encouragement comes from believing the simple truth of the incarnation – God is with us.[14]

The question may arise, 'How can I practically build a relationship with God that increases my belief in His presence in my life?' The greatest source of building a friendship with God in my own life has been through daily time in the Word and in prayer. Since I was a teenager, spending time daily in God's Word has helped me to know God and understand His great love for me. He has spoken to me so clearly through His Word on so many occasions that

---

11 Psalm 27:8-10

12 Psalm 27:13

13 Psalm 68:5

14 Matthew 1:23

at times it seems as if it was written just for me! In prayer, I find myself entering into conversation with the Lord. Personally, I have found journaling the best way to pour out my heart to God. Each day, I write a simple letter (some days longer than others) to the Lord, putting before Him the cares of my heart, all the while learning to entrust my life to Him. I have boxes and shelves filled with old journals, all which speak to the most important relationship in my life. Walking with Him each day has profoundly affected every other relationship in my life. If you struggle to know how to study the Bible on your own, or when to find the time, I encourage you to seek out someone for advice or accountability. God uses others within our community to help us develop a rich devotional life.

Desire Rightly

This past week at church, we celebrated the Lord's Supper. At our church, everyone goes to the front to receive the sacrament, and usually during this time, I quietly bow my head in prayer and reflection. However, this week, I chose to keep my eyes open and watch the different people in our church walk up to receive the bread and the wine. I watched as dear friends walked by and also observed people whom I had never met. Known and unknown, here we all were, sharing in the grace of Christ together. It mattered little that I did not know their names; what mattered is that we both knew Christ. My favorite part of communion happens at the end when our Pastor serves the elements to our elders. Those who had been giving the sacrament now sit down to receive it. Once our Pastor gets to the end of the line and has distributed the meal to all of our elders, he exchanges places with the final elder, who stands and serves communion to the seated Pastor. To me, this exemplifies the beauty of true community: people coming together in service to one another, yet also being served. This ceremony demonstrates the union of God's people, sharing in the body and blood of their Savior. It also reminds me that if we want to put away our incorrect and idolatrous desires in relationships, we need to put on new, correct desires.

One place to begin to understand what we should desire relationally is to look at Jesus and His apostles. What did Jesus desire relationally? In Luke's Gospel, we hear the answer to this question in Jesus' own words. He speaks to the disciples, saying, 'I have eagerly desired to eat this Passover with you before I suffer.' The Greek term translated here as 'desired,' *epithumeo*, is the same term translated as 'coveting' in reference to a sinful desire. This reference is the only time that Jesus uses this word in all of Scripture, and it comes as He discusses His rightful longing for communion with those whom He loves on the eve of His death. Jesus desired deep and intimate relationships. He left His followers with a meal that they would be able to celebrate in remembrance of Himself, with a promise that He would be with them as they celebrated. In communion, Jesus meets with His people, as they meet with each other.

Following in His stead, we should greatly desire communion with God's people. We should long for the church and join regularly with God's people in worship. Yes, the church is an imperfect and often-stained bride. Many people today consider themselves 'church wounded' and have decided to forego a relationship with the church as an institution. However, God established the church as His bride, and Jesus gave us a meal to celebrate within the context of the church. No church is perfect and at times there are good reasons to leave a particular congregation. However, each of us needs to find a place to worship God with other believers. Jesus desired to be in fellowship with His disciples at the Last Supper in spite of the fact that He knew one disciple would betray Him and *all* the rest would deny Him. His desire for community can be an example to each of us concerning where to begin our quest for intimate relationships with others. Being in the church does not mean that we will be insulated from painful relationships. However, it is our only hope for establishing healthy ones. Thus, we should desire greatly to develop and foster relationships within the church.

Secondly, we should desire our closest relationships to result from and share in gospel ministry. Paul's relational depth with the church at Philippi was born out of their shared work on behalf of the gospel. Paul prays for the Philippians with joy 'because of your partnership in the gospel from the first day until now, being confident of this, that he who began a good work in you will carry it on to completion until the day of Christ Jesus.'[15] He continues by stating, 'God can testify how I long for all of you with the affection of Christ Jesus.'[16] Paul deeply and intimately loved the Philippian believers. He did not attempt to protect himself from deep relationships with others by claiming a relationship so intimate with Christ that he had no need for other relationships. Instead, it is the depth of his relationship with Christ that spurred on his love and longing for deep relationships with other believers. However, his longing and love for them was based on a shared commitment to seeing Christ proclaimed in all things. He wanted for them their best good, which he expressed as he prayed, 'that your love may abound more and more in knowledge and depth of insight, so that you may be able to discern what is best and may be blameless until the day of Christ, filled with the fruit of righteousness that comes through Jesus Christ – to the glory and praise of God.'[17]

When we consider friendships, our hope in them should be that we spur one another on in the faith. The place for the greatest depth in relationship comes from a shared

15 Philippians 1:4-6

16 Philippians 1:8

17 Philippians 1:9-11

commitment to knowing Christ and proclaiming Him to others. If you long to have greater depth with others, you must long for relationships that will spur you on in the faith, not simply someone to join you for a movie on Friday evening. We must desire *more* in relationships, not less, if we want to find true satisfaction in them. The greatest relationships we find will be based in a shared commitment to Christ and a shared hope to live lives worthy of His gospel. This truth does not mean that we do not have genuine friendship with non-Christians in our lives. However, they will not be able to share in the truest part of ourselves with us, so in some sense they will always be lacking a depth and intimacy that we can share with our Christian friends. As we desire this type of intimacy, we must be prepared to love self-sacrificially as we enter into relationship with others.

Give Generously

A woman seeking Christ while desiring deep and intimate friendships within the context of the church must also be prepared to give generously in friendship. As she takes off her negative pattern of taking from others, she will need to give to others freely, gracefully and sacrificially. A woman who gives freely to others supports them when they are in need and looks out for their best interests. She sees others' gifts and talents and praises them, hoping to encourage them on in their pursuits. She rejoices when her friend rejoices and mourns when she mourns. She is secure enough in her relationship with Christ that she does not cling to the friendship, but rather treasures the friend. For over twenty years, my friend Beth and I have shared life together. We met in high school and then went on to be roommates for all four years of college. Our hair and clothing began to look so similar that at times people would get us confused and call us by the other's name. Since college, we have lived in different cities and literally been separated at times by an ocean of miles. Each of us has made new friends and shared intimate fellowship with others in our churches, neighborhoods and jobs. Yet, we have always remained committed to one another and our friendship. However, our relationship has always felt incredibly free from all forms of jealousy or envy. I am glad she has a playgroup of moms with whom she shares the joys of motherhood. I rejoice in the fact that she is in a church with godly women and excellent Bible studies. She is no less my friend because she has other friends. Yet, I treasure her friendship because I know that in the time it takes to make a phone call, I can share with her my life, my struggles and my joys and know she will listen and support me prayerfully. Our freedom in friendship may mean that at times we go for months without talking, but that because of Christ, we are always sharing in each others lives, no matter how far apart we live.

Secondly, a woman will give gracefully as she enters into friendships with other women. Like Joseph, she will be able to forgive others, because she knows how much she has been forgiven. She will not expect perfection, but will speak words of grace. She will trust her friend instead of being suspicious or constantly insecure. She will not manipulate to get others to do what she wants, but she will prayerfully consider how she can encourage her friends on towards love and good deeds.

Thirdly, a woman must be prepared to give sacrificially as she enters into friendships with others. She enters into friendship seeking to love others as she has been loved by Christ. She pursues others instead of waiting to be pursued. She listens to their concerns and faithfully prays for her friends. She uses her time to write a note of encouragement instead of watching TV or surfing the Internet. A woman who gives freely, gracefully and sacrificially will rarely be without intimate friends. It is not through taking that we find the relationships we desire; it is by following in the way of Christ and giving to others, even at cost to ourselves.

CONFESS FREELY

Lastly, in order to weed out our covetous relational desires, we need to confess freely our struggles in this area. At times, simply admitting that we are clinging to our friendships or family relationships instead of to Christ is the first step in letting go of this form of idolatry. Coming to the realization that we are expecting from our children, parents, grandparents, pastors or friends what only Christ can fully provide is essential to learning how to gracefully share life with those closest to us. We also must be willing to lovingly confront our friends and family when we see them caught in relational idolatry. It does not truly help a friend to simply commiserate with them about their difficult boss, hurtful friend or self-absorbed sister. We must be faithful to listen and pray, but also faithful to point them to Christ's love and encourage them to share that love in difficult relationships. As the world watches us giving freely, gracefully and sacrificially in friendships, surely they will notice the free grace of Christ, given sacrificially for each of us.

Questions for Personal Reflection and Group Discussion

1. What are different ways that we define friendships from childhood through adulthood? How do we seek security and love in our friendships?
2. Consider the story of Joseph, beginning with his grandparents, Isaac and Rebekah. How do you see the effects of relational jealousy and favoritism throughout the generations?
3. Read Genesis 37. How do you observe the pattern of 'see, covet, take and hide' in this passage?
4. What consequences did the brothers live with after their actions? See also Genesis 42:21.

5. Read Genesis 50:19-21. How did Joseph's gracious response to the relational harm he suffered differ from his brother's earlier response to their father's favoritism? How did his forgiveness end years of painful relational conflicts?
6. Can you think of painful family relationships that have persisted over several generations? How can jealousy and envy lead to family disputes that span decades?
7. How can coveting and envy take from our friendships with others? How does an envious friend drain the friendships she has?
8. Read Psalm 27:8-10. How is a relationship with the Lord different from all earthly relationships? What are some ways we can cultivate our relationship with the Lord?
9. Why do some people feel wounded by the church? Why is the church a necessary community in the life of a Christian?
10. Read Philippians 1:4-11. How would you characterize Paul's friendship with the Philippians? What is his hope for them? How does that compare to your hopes in friendship?
11. Can you think of a time when you built a friendship with someone as you served together in some way? How did that deepen the friendship?
12. What is the problem in seeking fulfillment in our earthly relationships? How does it cause us harm and prevent us from loving others sacrificially?
13. Consider your current friendships. How might God desire healthier patterns in those relationships? With whom could you be more encouraging or a better listener? Who could you serve without expecting any service in return? Who do you need to forgive or show mercy?

8 *Coveting Seasons and Circumstances*

God carries his children through this world through a variety of conditions. Sometimes we lack, and at other times we abound. This allows our graces to be tested. We will find that God's love is stable, certain, and constant in a variety of conditions. God does not change, and his love is constant however our lives might change. We must learn not to quarrel with God's government. Let God do as he pleases as he brings us to heaven. It is no matter what the way is like, or how rugged it is, as long as he brings us there. God's grace is able to carry his children above all our conditions.

RICHARD SIBBES

Voices From the Past, p. 323.

8

Coveting Seasons and Circumstances:

The Story of the Israelites

A few years ago, I remember being at a social gathering and speaking to my friend Elisabeth.[1] She was in her mid-thirties and struggling with contentment after a long season of singleness. Her heart, gradually encrusted with bitterness, led her to quickly see everyone else's blessings, while focusing in on her own struggles. I attempted to speak into her life, explaining that most people, even those married, were also struggling with contentment in some area. At that moment, she spotted a mutual friend, Amanda, who was cuddling with her new baby. She turned to me and claimed, 'Well, see, Amanda has finally gotten it all. She's been hoping for a baby and now she's finally content.' I remained silent, realizing that I was unable to share with her the irony of her choice. Just a few weeks before her due date, Amanda's husband had confessed his unfaithfulness, which led to a variety of painful consequences. While Amanda visited with other women at the party, cuddling her much-hoped-for little boy, she was struggling each day with the

1 All names have been changed.

painful repercussions of her husband's actions. However, their struggle was private, and known to only a few friends.

This experience spoke volumes to me regarding the danger of looking over the fence and comparing our life stage or circumstances with another woman's situation. We simply cannot compare, because we do not know what hides behind an attractive smile or seemingly perfect family. As I have met with women and heard their stories, I have become increasingly convinced that we are all trudging through a broken existence. Some circumstances are surely more painful than others, but in truth, we simply cannot know where our own set of difficulties fall on the continuum. All we can know for certain is that the seasons or circumstances in which we find ourselves are ordained by our loving Father with the promised intent of making us into the image of His Son.

In this chapter, we will explore the danger of coveting different life stages or seasons of life, as well as particular circumstances within our given season. For instance, the woman struggling as a mother of multiple young children might be tempted to covet her single friend's free time. Or, she might look to the next stage, believing that once all of her children are in elementary school, then she will be in a much more manageable season of life. It is easy to see how we can believe that we will find abundant life when we reach the next stage of life or if we could just go back in time to a season when life was less complicated. We can also be guilty of coveting within our own season as we compare our circumstances to those around us. The same mom of young children might also covet the lives of her friends in a similar season because she views their circumstances as easier to manage. Perhaps they have greater financial resources to provide babysitters, cleaning help, or a reliable car. Maybe their husbands work different hours or travel less. Whatever situation, it can become easy to wrongly believe that contentment is found in a different season of life or a different set of circumstances.

The Israelites provide ample examples to us of our propensity towards this type of coveting. While roaming in the desert, they regularly complained about their season of wandering, even desiring the misery of returning to slavery in Egypt. Once they finally came into their own land and became a nation, they suddenly found that they wanted to be just like all the other nations and have a king, despite warnings that a king would harm their prosperity. In observing and exploring the Israelites' coveting in both of these ways and the consequences they bore, we will find great warning against this type of inordinate desire.

They Saw

The Israelites spent hundreds of years enslaved in Egypt. During this time, they were pressed into forced labor, lived bitter lives and used ruthlessly by the Egyptians.[2] At one point, because of their increasing numbers, the king of Egypt ordered that all the baby boys be thrown into the Nile.[3] The Israelites' suffering was great, and they called out to God in their distress, hoping for redemption from slavery. In His faithfulness, God answered and brought them out, allowing them to see firsthand all that His power could accomplish.

The Israelites saw many miraculous events as they escaped from the Egyptians. They witnessed the Lord bringing plague after plague upon Egypt. They observed with wonder as the Red Sea was parted and they crossed safely on dry land. They also watched as the Sea closed back, crushing the entire Egyptian army. In response to this victory, Moses and the Israelites sang a song, worshipping the Lord.[4] Even though their eyes had seen these miraculous events, just

---

2 Exodus 1:11-14

3 Exodus 1:22

4 Exodus 15:1

three days later they despaired and grumbled before Moses because they could not find water. By their second month of wandering, they could only recall an unrealistic view of their past, lamenting, 'If only we had died by the LORD's hand in Egypt! There we sat around pots of meat and ate all the food we wanted, but you have brought us out into this desert to starve this entire assembly to death.'[5] Their unbelief led them to a false view of their past and brought about an inability to see their current situation with eyes of faith.

This unfaithful view of their circumstances reached a pinnacle when the twelve spies returned with their report about the Promised Land. The spies described that the land did indeed flow with milk and honey, but that all the people who lived there were powerful. Ten of these men, filled with unbelief, spread a bad report, saying:

> The land we explored devours those living in it. All the people we saw there are of great size. We saw the Nephilim there [the descendants of Anak come from the Nephilim]. We seemed like grasshoppers in our own eyes, and we looked the same to them.[6]

Their eyes were full of the reality of the physical situation. In contrast, Caleb and Joshua, seeing the reality of their situation through the eyes of faith, boldly stated:

> The land we passed through and explored is exceedingly good. If the LORD is pleased with us, he will lead us into that land, a land flowing with milk and honey, and will give it to us. Only do not rebel against the LORD. And do not be afraid of the people of the land, because we will swallow them up. Their protection is gone, but the LORD is with us. Do not be afraid of them.[7]

---

5 Exodus 16:3

6 Numbers 13:32-33

7 Numbers 14:7-9

Here we see clearly that the exact same circumstances can be viewed differently simply because of belief. Caleb and Joshua, choosing to walk by faith and not by sight, had clearer vision than the other ten spies who were blinded by their unbelief.

Fearful of entering the Promised Land, and weary of their current wandering, the Israelites once again turned their eyes to their past in Egypt. Rather than reject the slavery of the past season, remembering its suffering and difficulties, they plotted together to choose a new leader and return to Egypt. Their eyes feared the next season, despaired in their current season and incorrectly remembered the previous season. Their inner unbelief allowed them to interpret all their circumstances without hope in the Lord's ability to fulfill all His promises. This failure to trust the Lord resulted in their desires becoming covetous.

They Coveted

In this situation, the Israelites' desire to return to Egypt was clearly covetous because it was against what the Lord had called them to pursue. The Lord called them out of the slavery of Egypt in order to bring them into the land He promised Abraham. Desiring to return to Egypt was a rejection of the Lord's plan. It was also clearly foolish to desire to return to a season full of pain and misery. The fact that they could so quickly forget God's kind dispensations towards them, as well as forget all the evil that the Egyptians had brought upon them, displayed the hardness of their hearts. They also failed to rejoice in the current provision of manna and quail and instead focused on the pots of meat they had while living in Egypt. Blinded by unbelief, their desires turned towards paths that would only lead to more suffering.

They Took

As the ten spies returned with their unfaithful advice, they led the other Israelites into their own unbelief and disobedience. Moses recounted, 'But you were unwilling to go up; you rebelled against the command of the LORD your God. You grumbled in your tents and said, "The Lord hates us; so he brought us out of Egypt to deliver us into the hands of the Amorites to destroy us. Where can we go? Our brothers have made us lose heart."'[8] The first negative result of the spies' own unbelief was that they caused others to lose heart. Their failure is a good warning for each of us as we face seasons and circumstances that seem beyond our ability to bear. Our own faith in the Lord's provision can inspire others towards similar faith. In contrast, our disbelief and despair about our circumstances can cause others to lose heart in their own situation.

The Israelites also took from Moses' leadership. First of all, they decided that they wanted a new leader, one who would take them back to Egypt. Then, as their grumbling increased, the whole assembly talked about stoning Moses, Aaron, Joshua and Caleb. Unrighteousness and unbelief are in perpetual war with faithfulness and obedience. In their sin, the Israelites were even willing to kill those who were living by faith.

They Hid

The Israelites hid their unbelief in two ways. First of all, they hid behind the difficulty of their known circumstances. Surely wandering in the desert with no end in sight was unpleasant. The people were fully dependent on the Lord to provide water and manna. When the spies returned and spoke of further difficulties, it was easy for them to simply throw their hands up in the air and say, 'Enough is enough! How can the Lord expect us to bear all of this?' Similarly, we are sometimes tempted to hide our inner unbelief behind the difficulties of our outer circumstances. However, it is in these dark and difficult moments that true faith shines

8 Deuteronomy 1:26-28

all the more clearly, precisely because of the surrounding darkness.

Secondly, the Israelites hid their covetous desires by claiming good motives for their disobedience. They claimed, 'Our wives and children will be taken as plunder. Wouldn't it be better for us to go back to Egypt?'[9] Certainly, the desire to protect one's family is a worthy one. However, one can provide no better protection for his family than a sure trust in and steadfast obedience to the Lord. To believe in any provision other than a faithful and careful adherence to the Lord's chosen path is a failure with great peril. While we are often tempted to hide our disobedience out of love for one another, it is never truly loving to walk in any way other than complete obedience to the Lord's call on our lives.

They Suffered Consequences

Once again, covetous desires led to painful consequences. The Israelites' desire to return to Egypt angered the Lord so greatly that He questioned Moses, 'How long will these people treat me with contempt? How long will they refuse to believe in me, in spite of all the miraculous signs I have performed among them? I will strike them down with a plague and destroy them, but I will make you into a nation greater and stronger than they.'[10] Moses appealed, not to the Israelites' innocence, but to God's glory, and begged Him to forgive their sin and rebellion. While God did forgive His people, He also punished them, saying, 'Not one of the men who saw my glory and the miraculous signs I performed in Egypt and in the desert but who disobeyed me and tested me ten times – not one of them will ever see the land I promised on oath to their forefathers. No one who has treated me with contempt will ever see it.'[11]

---

9 Numbers 14:3

10 Numbers 14:11-12

11 Numbers 14:22-23

The Israelites' season of wandering in the wilderness was extended forty years because of their unfaithful desire to return to Egypt. Of this generation of Israelites, only Caleb and Joshua were allowed to enter into the Promised Land. In a similar way, our covetous seasonal and circumstantial desires demonstrate contempt for the Lord. We need to recognize that at times, more painful circumstances will result because of our grumbling and discontent in the current season the Lord has placed us. Before we look at the consequences we often bear, it will be necessary to explore this pattern of seasonal coveting in our own lives.

We See

Whenever we are in a particular season, it is always easy to see the benefits of another woman's season of life, while failing to consider or remember the struggles. The Israelites looked back to their time in Egypt and fondly remembered the pots of meat, forgetting the hard labor, the bitter treatment and the murder of their infants. They also saw and yearned for the Promised Land, but they wanted it to come without any struggle or effort.

We also share their ability to see our past seasons with rose-colored glasses and to view our current season as more difficult than we expected. We can fondly remember the fun and friendship of college years while forgetting the stress of exams and papers. The mother of young children can look ahead and believe that life will get much easier once all her children are in school each day, not realizing the added pressure that will come from transporting multiple children to different activities. The single woman can believe that her life will be so much more settled once she is married, falsely believing that simply knowing who she will spend her future with will make it more secure. The elderly woman looks back on the days when her body was free from aches and pains, longing to wake up in the morning and get out of bed with ease.

We can also see women in our same season and play the comparison game. The college student paying her way through school views those getting to experience college without working and wishes she could have that kind of freedom. The mother of twins views mothers of single children and believes her life would be so much simpler with only one child waking up in the middle of the night. The single woman who rarely gets asked out can look with envy upon another single lady in her church getting asked out regularly. The working mom can covet the stay-at-home mom's time with her children, while the stay-at-home mom desires the productivity she used to have while she worked. One woman's adult children stay close by, while another woman's move far away. In every season of life, we may see the lives of other women and begin to play the comparison game. Our seeing, mixed with unbelief in the Lord's goodness to us, will quickly turn into coveting.

We Covet

In every season, there are blessings and difficulties. Our unbelief towards God usually begins when we forget that every season has its share of trouble. In many ways, we should actually expect that life's circumstances will grow increasingly difficult. We live in a fallen world. The longer we are alive, the more we will experience brokenness in our own life and in the lives of others. This reality should lead us to long all the more for our heavenly home. However, in many cases it just increases our discontent and our striving to control our outward circumstances in an attempt to shield ourselves from the difficulties of life. Our coveting in this area demonstrates how firmly we believe in the promises of this world, instead of the life that can come only through an ever-growing relationship with Christ.

As we covet the comforts and blessings of another season, usually we desire what is rare in our own situation. When I had three small children at home, always desiring my attention, the thing I could find myself coveting the most was time alone. My days were spent with the constant demands of mothering, and often it was difficult to simply go to the bathroom by myself! I craved time alone – going to the grocery store, shopping for clothes, reading a book. When I observed my single friends getting to do these simple activities on their own, it was easy for me to sinfully desire their freedom. I loved my children dearly, but I wanted to be able to have them without losing the freedom I enjoyed at other stages. In truth, I wanted it all.

Each season has rarity. The single woman faces the longing for companionship, someone to share her life with day to day. The mother of young children desires freedom. The mother of older children desires the control she used to have over her children's friends and schedule. The working woman desires freedom from the stresses of her job, while the non-working woman desires the added income of a paycheck.

These rarities can also affect our covetous desires within our particular season. Some single women have wonderful friendships that ease their longing for companionship. Some married women have easier marriages. Some women's young children are more obedient and some women's older children seem to drift easily through adolescence. In every season, some women have more financial resources, encouraging family members, and other circumstances that appear to ease their difficulties in a particular season. However, we must always realize that we only see a limited view of the outward circumstances of another person's life. In truth, we are interpreting everything through our own, finite view of the world. God's view of all of our circumstances, and the circumstances of others, is complete and infinite in scope. He is weaving together a perfect story that will one day be told in full. When we covet in these circumstantial events, we are trusting in our own definition of goodness, rather than entrusting our lives to Him who works all things for our good.

Our coveting is most often displayed through our grumbling and complaining. Just like the Israelites, we moan about our current situation and forget the difficulties of other seasons. We become increasingly self-absorbed, seeking earthly ways to ease the difficulties instead of turning to the Lord of all of our circumstances. It is not coveting to be aware of the difficulties or struggles of our particular season; it is coveting to be full of bitterness and discontentment because of the difficulties. A content woman can share with friends and the Lord her honest struggle. However, she does so in a way that demonstrates her belief and trust in the Lord. In contrast, the covetous woman believes her outward circumstances are proof of the Lord's failure to be good to her. She complains and grumbles, seeking others to join her in her lament. She cultivates discontent and soon, she becomes a woman who takes from those around her.

We Take

Women who covet seasons and circumstances take in a variety of ways. First of all, they have difficulty extending friendship to anyone except those in their same season. The single woman coveting marriage quickly stops spending time with her married friends. She believes they cannot understand her struggles. Or, she may lose her married friends because her self-focus causes her to believe their lives are perfect now that they are married. She fails to listen to her married friends' struggles and her friendships become increasingly one-sided. Likewise, the mother of a rebellious teenager can only discuss her situation with mothers of other difficult teenagers. Rather than gain potential wisdom from a variety of friends, she isolates herself, believing that no one else can understand her struggle. We tend to stay locked into friendships with people who look just like us, missing out on the growth that could come from knowing women of different ages, stages, socio-economic backgrounds and circumstances.

Secondly, we take because we are unable to love our neighbor as Christ loved us. When we simply view our neighbor as a means of measuring ourselves, we will never care for him or her well. We will fixate on what is easier in that person's life and fail to sympathize or support what may be difficult for him or her. Our prayers will be centered on our own cares, instead of on those around us.

Finally, we take from others as we spread discontentment about our circumstances instead of radiating contentment. I recently heard a speaker talk about how discontentment was similar to a germ, spreading from one person to the next like a bad cold. As we focus on the daily struggles of our earthly circumstances, our example will encourage others to do the same. Placing our expectations in temporal longings leaves us hungry and wanting, and unable to give hope to others. We are like a starving man, opening his mouth trying to eat the wind. We find no satisfaction because we take in no true sustenance. Our own emptiness causes us to take from others in an attempt to fill ourselves. Once we have taken, we attempt to hide the reality of our discontentment from those around us.

We Hide

In our season of discontent, we usually hide in one of two ways. Some women attempt to hide by excusing themselves from their discontentment by explaining time and again the difficulty of a particular circumstance. Such a person hides her own sin as she thinks to herself, 'My situation is so uniquely difficult that I am allowed to be miserable. Anyone facing what I am facing would be just as discontent as I am.' Paul speaks to the fallacy of this type of thinking when he writes, 'No temptation has seized you except what is *common* to man. And God is faithful; he will not let you be tempted beyond what you can bear. But when you are tempted, he will also provide a way out so that you can stand up under it' (emphasis added).[12] Whatever we are facing is more common than we realize. While it is easy to hide our sin because of the difficulty of our circumstances, we must come out of our hiding place and confess if we want to find freedom. Otherwise, we may simply fall into a second type of hiding.

In contrast with outward grumbling, some women seek to hide their own discontentment by putting on an appearance of happiness. Inwardly, they are still comparing their circumstances with others and grumbling before the Lord. However, they keep all of this to themselves, quietly judging others around them and feeling disappointed with the Lord. This type of hiding separates them from other people and God. Rather than overflowing with life to others, they pull back and hide their true feelings. They are no less discontent; they are just attempting to hide the true state of their heart.

Our seeing, coveting, taking and hiding in the different seasons of our lives will bear consequences in our lives just as it did for the Israelites. We may miss out on blessings the Lord wants to give us in a particular season because we are so focused on what is lacking. Just as the Israelites were given forty extra years of wandering in the desert, we may experience additional hardships because of our grumbling and complaining. We need to fight this type of coveting by seeking the Lord, desiring rightly, giving generously and confessing freely so that we may joyfully accept the blessings of the season we are currently experiencing.

Seek the Lord

When we are facing difficult circumstances or seasons, it is tempting to try to find comfort from others facing similar trials or even from those who are facing more difficult

12 1 Corinthians 10:13

struggles. One day I came to the realization that, at times, I tried to gain contentment from the fact that someone else in the world was facing more dire circumstances than my own. This approach may be rooted in the common parenting line, 'You need to eat your vegetables – don't you know there are children starving in the world?' In a similar way, I would attempt to convince myself that I should have joy based on someone else's hardship. For instance, suppose I was having a difficult day for some reason. I might say to myself, 'Well, at least I don't live in Haiti and my house has just fallen down because of that terrible earthquake.' Of course, we can use world events to gain perspective on our situation, but it is quite a dangerous place to attempt to find contentment. The Scriptures never tell us to find our joy in the fact that our situation is not as unfortunate as possible. We are told to find our joy in the fact that all our circumstances flow from God's loving hand. One day, we may face the earthquake, flood, or other disaster that we once used to gain perspective. If we are holding onto our contentment because circumstances could be worse, what happens when our situation is more difficult than anyone else's we know? Comparing seasons and circumstances might provide perspective, but abiding joy flows from an ever-deepening affection for the Lord. Seeking the Lord throughout life's seasons and circumstances is the key to contentment in all things.

As we seek to know the Lord in our seasons, we need to remember a few truths about our circumstances. First of all, the Lord has called us to rejoice in them. Paul exhorts, 'Be joyful always; pray continually; give thanks in all circumstances, for this is God's will for you in Christ Jesus.'[13] Paul makes it clear that we are called to rejoice always and in all circumstances. Whatever season you are facing, there is a call to joy. Paul never says that all the circumstances

13 1 Thessalonians. 5:16-18

themselves are good. Christians face terrible hardships and experience evil acts wrongfully committed against them. We do not rejoice in man's evil acts or delight in the brokenness of this world. We rejoice in the God who is able and willing to redeem and use these difficulties for good. This basis for joy leads us to the second truth we need to cling to and believe about our circumstances.

If we want to find contentment and joy, we must put on the belief that God is bringing forth and providentially reigning over all that comes into our lives. God, speaking through Isaiah, says, 'Listen to me…you whom I have upheld since you were conceived, and have carried since your birth. Even to your old age and gray hairs I am he, I am he who will sustain you.'[14] From conception to death, the Lord is intimately, kindly and thoughtfully sustaining those He loves. He continues discussing His complete power over all His creation when He proclaims, 'I am God, and there is none like me. I make known the end from the beginning, from ancient times, what is still to come. I say: My purpose will stand, and I will do all that I please. From the east I summon a bird of prey; from a far-off land, a man to fulfill my purpose. What I have said, that will I bring about; what I have planned, that will I do.'[15] While it may appear to our eyes that everything swirling about us is completely random and out of control, we must remember that all events are subject to God's careful planning. He is writing a beautiful story that will one day be told in fullness and much rejoicing. In each of us, He is constantly at work for our good, making us into the image of His Son.[16] Often, we will not see with our own understanding on this side of eternity all the ways He is working all things for good. We must each choose, like Caleb and Joshua, to see

14 Isaiah 46:3-4

15 Isaiah 46:9b-10

16 Romans 8:28-29

with the eyes of faith and believe that God is at work in our particular season, making us and forming us in more loving ways than we would have even known to ask.

Ecclesiastes speaks to the different seasons each of us encounter. Solomon proclaims, 'There is a time for everything, and a season for every activity under heaven: a time to be born and a time to die, a time to plant and a time to uproot.'[17] After listing many of the circumstances we all face, he concludes, 'He has made everything beautiful in its time. He has also set eternity in the hearts of men; yet they cannot fathom what God has done from beginning to end.'[18] In our finiteness, we simply cannot understand the workings of an infinite God. David proclaimed it in the Psalms: 'Such knowledge is too wonderful for me, too lofty for me to attain.'[19] While we cannot always understand the workings of God, we can believe that He is always working to make everything beautiful in its time.

Our belief in His providence allows us to trust in Him and discipline ourselves to stop comparing our stories with those around us. In C.S. Lewis' fictional story, *The Horse and His Boy*, young Shasta finally meets the lion, Aslan, the God-figure of the series. Aslan describes how he has been following Shasta all of his life and was with him along every path. At one point, Shasta questions Aslan's dealing with his friend Aravis. Aslan responds, 'Child, I am telling you your story, not hers. I tell no one any story but his own.'[20] We need to seek the Lord, observe His work in our own story, and let go of comparing our lot with someone else's.

Lastly, we need to believe that whatever the circumstances or difficulties that come into our lives, the mercies of God

17 Ecclesiastes 3:1-2

18 Ecclesiastes 3:11

19 Psalm 139:6

20 C.S. Lewis, *The Horse and His Boy*, (New York: HarperCollins, 1954), p. 165.

far outweigh the afflictions. It can be easy to discount all that we have as we set our eyes on what is lacking. In every season and circumstance, we need to remember the wealth that is ours in Christ. *The Rare Jewel of Christian Contentment* says it this way:

> Though I cannot know what your afflictions are, yet I know what your mercies are, and I know they are so great that I am sure there can be no afflictions in this world as great as the mercies you have. If it were only this mercy, that you have this day of grace and salvation continued to you: it is a greater mercy than any affliction. Set any affliction beside this mercy and see which would weigh the heaviest; this is certainly greater than any affliction. That you have the day of grace and salvation, that you are not now in hell, this is a greater mercy.[21]

We need to allow the reality of Christ's mercy for us to invade all areas of our life and fill us anew with the joy of our redemption and salvation. In focusing on His mercy, we will find a contentment and joy that will give abundance in every season.

Desire Rightly

As we spend time with the Lord each day, slowly our desires will transform and grow into new hopes. Even as we long for circumstances to change, our greater longing will be for contentment in any and every circumstance. We hold our hopes before the Lord, trusting in Him to fulfill them in His timing. During one particular season of waiting in my own life, I came across Psalm 32:9: 'Do not be like the horse or the mule, which have no understanding but must be controlled by bit and bridle or they will not come to you.' As I read this verse, I realized that it described my own unwillingness to submit my life to the Lord's clear leading. I was

21 Jeremiah Burroughs, *The Rare Jewel of Christian Contentment*, (Edinburgh: Banner of Truth Trust, 1964), p. 173.

acting like a mule – stubborn, willful and hard-hearted. I was following where the Lord wanted me to go, but I was failing to do it joyfully. Instead, I was being pulled along, fighting the reigns that were leading me in good paths. In that moment, the Lord was faithful to convict me and give me a better desire. My circumstances did not change, but the Lord gave me the new longing to come to Him in humbleness and meekness, rather than by the force of bit and bridle. What I believed I needed, He replaced with more of Himself, to show me again that He is my true sustenance. St. Augustine says it this way: 'How suddenly comforting it was to lose the false comforts of the past! I had long feared losing them, and now it was a joy to throw them away. Truly it was you who put them far from me, my true and supreme comfort; you put them far away and set yourself in their place.' Our desire in each season must begin with the quest to know God more fully in whatever set of circumstances He has placed us.

As we seek to desire well, it is helpful to take two perspectives as we deal with the difficulties of our season. First of all, we need to take a short view, asking ourselves, 'Can I bear this struggle for today?' Stop looking to next week, next month or next year. Simply get through *this* day. Usually, we can bear any struggle for one day. It is when we begin to borrow trouble, wondering how long we must endure a particular trial, that we can become overwhelmed by our circumstances. No one knows how long a hardship will last. Our goal is to simply trust God to help us today, because each day has enough worry of its own.[22]

Secondly, we need to take a long view of our circumstance, asking ourselves, 'In light of eternity, can I consider this trial light and momentary?' As we meditate upon the weight of glory that will be ours in heaven, we can endure much waiting here. Our children can tolerate many hours in the

---

22 Matthew 6:34

car journeying to the beach, because they believe fun-filled days await them. As we journey through different seasons, we must keep our eyes on our heavenly destination when the traveling becomes tiring. As we focus on what will be ours in heaven, we find hope here on earth.

Give Generously

As we seek the Lord, and He gives us new desires, we will become women who give generously in every season. The first Psalm speaks to this truth when it describes the man who delights in the law of the Lord. The Psalmist declares, 'He is like a tree planted by streams of water, which yields its fruit in season and whose leaf does not wither. Whatever he does prospers.'[23] Psalm 92 continues this analogy, saying, 'They will still bear fruit in old age, they will stay fresh and green.'[24] Those planted firmly by the pure water of Scripture will bear fruit that overflows in every season.

What fruit does a woman abiding in the Lord bear in every season? Paul tells us that the fruit of the Spirit is, 'love, joy, peace, patience, kindness, goodness, faithfulness, gentleness and self-control.'[25] In every season, walking by the Spirit, we can abound in these attributes. In doing so, we will give generously to everyone we meet. This description of the fruit of the Spirit is a picture of contentment. Our personal contentment wells up into springs of generosity towards others.

Women who give generously in their particular season will most likely be women who have friendships that span different life stages. They seek to give understanding to other women in a different set of circumstances, and share their lives with those who may not completely understand their own struggles. One of my closest relationships has

---

23 Psalm 1:3

24 Psalm 92:14

25 Galatians 5:22-23

grown over the years with my friend, Angela. I originally met her when she moved to town and began babysitting for my children. Eventually, she started attending a Bible study at our home, and then we began meeting regularly for prayer. Through the years, she has watched me go from having one young child to a busy family of three children. She has played chase or hide-n-seek and read more children's books than most single women in their twenties. She has been generous to give her time to us so that my husband and I could enjoy peaceful date nights. We have spent hours together preparing for ministry outreaches, writing Bible studies or simply cooking meals in my kitchen. Our differing seasons have actually been a blessing to each of us in a variety of ways. Angela's generosity has blessed her with three young children who race to the door with hugs and love to shower upon her the moment she walks in our home. She has also gained perspective on her own life stage by sharing life with our family. She sees more clearly the blessings of her own season as she observes some of the difficulties of motherhood. In a similar way, I see more clearly the many blessings of my family, as I observe the difficulties of being a single woman in her late twenties. Giving generously in our stages allows for the body of Christ to work well and bless each member. What is lacking in one season can be shared by another woman in a different season.

Confess Freely

As we struggle in our seasons and circumstances, we must be women who confess freely. In my current season of working part-time and mothering full-time, I sometimes wrongly believe that if I just had more hours in the day, then I would be content. My covetous desire for time to myself can lead me to grow inwardly discontent when I hear that someone else went to a movie or spent a weekend alone in the mountains. Rather than sit and stew in my frustration, I need to confess it – both to God and to women who will faithfully pray for me. Hiding my resentment will simply allow it to pop up in other ways and will cause me to miss out on the blessings of others' faithful prayers. We all struggle in certain areas with the Lord's call upon our lives. We need to confess our weakness so that He will fill us with belief, allowing us to proclaim, 'LORD, you have assigned me my portion and my cup; you have made my lot secure. The boundary lines have fallen for me in pleasant places; surely I have a delightful inheritance.'[26] We must pray for eyes of faith that observe clearly the wealth that is ours in Christ throughout every season of life.

Questions for Personal Reflection and Group Discussion

1. Have you ever believed one particular woman 'had it all' in life? What led you to draw that conclusion? What is the fallacy of making such claims about someone else's life?

2. How can fostering relationships with women in different seasons of life be difficult? How can it be a blessing?

3. Read Exodus 1:11-14, 22 and Exodus 16:3. How did the Israelites' perspective while wandering in the wilderness lead them to falsely remember their past suffering? What are ways we romanticize past experiences (or future ones) and fail to see the good of our current situation?

4. Read Numbers 13:26–14:4. How does the inner unbelief of the Israelites cause them to interpret all their circumstances without hope? What is the difference between Caleb and Joshua and the other ten spies? How did the Israelites attempt to hide their lack of faith?

26 Psalm 16:5-6

5. Read Numbers 14:22-24. What consequences befell the Israelites?
6. How do we easily see the benefits of another person's life stage? How do we compare the struggles of our particular season with other women in different seasons? How does this comparison game lead us to envy and jealousy?
7. How does coveting in this way lead to disunity in the body of Christ? Do you have friendships that cross ages and stages, or are most of your friends exactly in the same season as you? Why or why not?
8. How does each season of life have both blessings *and* hardships? Consider the different seasons of a woman's life – what blessings are in each season and what hardships accompany each season?
9. How do we also compare with others in our similar season or life stage? How does this comparison lead us to take from others and fail to love others as Christ loved us?
10. Read 1 Corinthians 10:13. How does this verse expose the fallacy of the belief that the uniqueness of our situation allows us to grumble, complain or be bitter?
11. What is the difference between comparing our situation to someone who has it *more* difficult than us to finding contentment and entrusting our circumstances to the Lord to find contentment?
12. Read 1 Thessalonians 5:16-18. For what reason are we commanded to be joyful always? What is the difference in rejoicing in our circumstances versus rejoicing in the God who is in control of all our circumstances?
13. Why is the following statement, quoted at the beginning of this chapter, true? 'Though I cannot

know what your afflictions are, yet I know what your mercies are, and I know they are so great that I am sure there can be no afflictions in this world as great as the mercies you have.'

14. Read Psalm 32:9. Can you think of a time in your life when you struggled to entrust your circumstances to God and follow Him wholeheartedly? What does it look like to come to God by bit and bridle? What does it look like to come to God with a trustful heart?
15. How are our circumstances and seasons God's invitation for us to know Him in new ways? How can you see your depth of relationship with God correspond to the seasons and circumstances you have come through?
16. In what ways can we take both 'short view' and a 'long view' of our circumstances to help us endure difficult seasons in our lives?

9 *Coveting Giftedness and Abilities*

It is dangerous to do what we are not called to do, or to neglect our duty. The earth could not bear with Korah and swallowed him up. The sea bore witness against Jonah the runaway prophet. The ruin of many souls breaks in upon them at this door. We are judged for our own stewardship, and not that of another. God only requires faithfulness in our place. We do not find fault with an apple tree if it is laden with apples and not figs. It is an erratic spirit that carries men out of their place and calling. They may be proud and discontent with the place God has set them. The whole world is too narrow a walk for a proud heart. Shall they be hid in a crowd when they can show the world their worth? No, they cannot stand it. But man always prospers better in his own soil.

William Gurnall

Voices From the Past, p. 352

9

Coveting Giftedness and Abilities:

The Story of Korah

One of my favorite children's books, *The Little Rabbit Who Wanted Red Wings,* begins in the following way:

> Once upon a time there was a little White Rabbit with two beautiful pink ears and two bright red eyes and four soft little feet – SUCH a pretty little white rabbit, but he wasn't happy. Just think, this little White Rabbit wanted to be somebody else instead of the nice little rabbit that he was.[1]

Whenever one of the forest animals would pass, the little White Rabbit would notice some special feature and tell his mother, 'Oh, mummy, I WISH I had...' whatever characteristic which made that animal special. He wanted Mr. Bushy Tail's long gray tail, Mr. Porcupine's back full of bristles, and Miss Puddle-Duck's lovely red webbed feet. As the story progresses, the wise Mr. Ground Hog tells the little White Rabbit that if he goes to the Wishing Pond and turns around three times, he will get whatever he wishes. He rushes off to the pond and just as he gets there, he spies a little red

1 Carolyn Sherwin Bailey, *The Little Rabbit Who Wanted Red Wings* (New York: Platt & Munk Publishers, 1931).

bird sitting on the edge of the pond. He turns around three times and wishes, 'Oh, I wish I had a pair of red wings!' Immediately, he begins to feel the wings start to grow and by the end of the day, he has a pair of beautiful, long red wings. He races home to show his mother, but when he gets there, he finds to his dismay that she does not recognize him and will not let him in the house. He returns to Mr. Ground Hog's home and sleeps uncomfortably all night on beechnuts. In the morning, as the little White Rabbit tries to use his wings to fly, he lands in a bush full of prickles and cries out to his mommy for help. Old Mr. Ground Hog comes to his rescue and asks how he feels about his new red wings. To the White Rabbit's dismay, the red wings have not brought him joy, but misery. Mr. Ground Hog encourages the little rabbit to simply go back to the well and wish them off again. The little White Rabbit does just that, and the story ends:

> Then he went home to his Mummy, who knew him right away and was so glad to see him; and the little White Rabbit never, NEVER, again wished to be something different from what he really was.

I have always loved this story. My mother read it to me, and I read it to my own children. It portrays so accurately how we tend to look at one another's gifts and abilities and want them as our own. Instead of a bushy tail, webbed feet or back full of bristles, we long for someone else's creativity, musical talents, intelligence, personality, or spiritual gifts. We fail to see our own unique qualities, and we desire the blessings God has given to someone else. In this chapter, we will look in detail at how our covetous desires for giftedness and abilities rob us of contentment. We will begin by studying the Old Testament story concerning Korah's jealousy of Aaron's priesthood. After looking at his example, we will turn inward and examine this covetous pattern in our own hearts. Finally, we will conclude by considering the truths about God that we need to put on in order to fight these covetous tendencies.

The Envy of Korah

Korah lived during the time of the Exodus. He was the son of Izhar, who was from the tribe of Levi. Izhar's brother was Amram, who was the father to Moses and Aaron.[2] Thus, Korah was a cousin to both Moses and Aaron and was a fellow Levite with them. The Levites were not included in the census of the Israelites, nor were they included in the distribution of land in Canaan. Instead, they were charged with the care of the tabernacle as the Israelites wandered in the desert. Only Levites could carry the ark, the furnishings, the tents, and any articles included in the tabernacle.[3] In return for their faithful service, the Lord gave them all the tithes in Israel as their inheritance.[4]

Each of the descendants of Levi had specific functions within the care of the tabernacle. Levi had three sons: Gershon, Kohath and Merari. The clans of Gershon were to care for the outer coverings of the tabernacle and the tent. The clans of Kohath were charged with caring for the ark, the table, the lampstand, the altars, and all the articles inside the sanctuary. The clans of Merari were responsible for taking care of the frames of the tabernacle, its crossbars, posts, bases, tent pegs and ropes.[5] Each Levitical family had specific duties given so that the tabernacle would remain sacred and set apart for the glory of God.

While each of the Levitical clans had special functions, Aaron and his sons were given the specific role as priests for the people of Israel. Only Aaron and his sons were consecrated to act as mediators between God and His people.

---

2 Exodus 6:16-21

3 Numbers 1: 47-53

4 Numbers 18:21

5 Numbers 3: 21-37

Specifically, they were the only ones sanctioned to put fire on the altar and present the different types of offerings to the Lord.[6] With this responsibility came both privileges and duties. The offerings must be performed according to the Scriptures, or else the priest would die. The day after the first offering was given in the desert, two of Aaron's sons, Nadab and Abihu, took their censers and put fire in them, along with incense. As they offered unauthorized fire before the Lord, fire came out from the presence of the Lord and consumed them. Aaron experienced the painful loss of two of his sons because they failed to obey the Lord's command with precision.[7]

However, the priesthood also came with special privileges. The Lord allowed for the priests to receive special portions of meat, grain, oil and bread as they ministered before the people. Only Aaron and his sons were allowed to eat these items, because they were holy. Aaron was also given sacred garments to wear as he ministered in the temple. He wore an ephod of linen, a breastpiece inlaid with precious stones, a woven tunic, a robe, a turban and a sash.[8] Both his food and his attire were set apart from the rest of the community of Israel.

Most likely, it was Aaron's special calling and privileges that led to Korah's profound envy. In Numbers 16, he and three other men rise up in rebellion against Moses and Aaron. Their insolence encouraged 250 other Israelite leaders to rebel, saying, 'You have gone too far! The whole community is holy, every one of them, and the LORD is with them. Why then do you set yourselves above the LORD's assembly?'[9] Moses fell on his face before Korah and his followers and told each of them to come to the tabernacle

---

6 Leviticus 1:7

7 Leviticus 10

8 Exodus 28

9 Numbers 16:3

in the morning. Then they could put censers with fire and incense before the LORD and see for themselves whom the LORD would choose. He specifically warned Korah:

> Now listen, you Levites! Isn't it enough for you that the God of Israel has separated you from the rest of the Israelite community and brought you near himself to do the work at the LORD's tabernacle and to stand before the community and minister to them? He has brought you and all your fellow Levites near himself, *but now you are trying to get the priesthood too*. It is against the LORD that you and all your followers have banded together. Who is Aaron that you should grumble against him? (emphasis added)[10]

The next morning, Korah and his followers appeared before the Lord and presented 250 censers of fire and incense. Through Moses, the Lord told everyone to move away from Korah and two of the other rebellious leaders. Immediately, the ground beneath them split apart, swallowed their households, all of their possessions, and buried them alive.[11] Afterwards, fire came out from the Lord and consumed the 250 men who had offered up fire and incense wrongly before the Lord. The Lord commanded Eleazar, son of Aaron, to take the censers and hammer them out over the altar as a reminder that only the descendants of Aaron should burn incense before the Lord.

Korah Saw

As we consider Korah's story, once again we can observe the same covetous pattern taking hold of his heart and leading to harmful consequences. Korah was part of the tribe of Levi and set apart for special service in the community of Israel. He was part of the Kohath clan and specifically was in charge of the most sacred items in the temple. However, he

---

10 Numbers 16: 8-11

11 Numbers 16: 31-33

was not a priest. Rather than seeing the special calling that the Lord had given him, he chose to focus on the unique calling of the priesthood. He saw that Aaron had a distinctive role in the service of Israel, and he wanted it for himself. Perhaps he saw the sacrifices Aaron was allowed to eat or the jeweled breastplate that he wore and wanted those for himself. We know from Korah's words that he believed he was just as holy as Aaron. The term 'holy' refers to being set apart. In this sense, Aaron was specifically set apart for the priesthood. It did not mean that Aaron was without personal sins, but that God had consecrated him for this particular task. Korah saw the distinction given to Aaron and rebelled against the Lord.

Korah Coveted

Psalm 106 recounts the Lord's enduring love for the Israelites, despite their many failings. As it traces the history of specific instances of Israel's disobedience, it comes to the story of Korah, explaining, 'In the camp they grew *envious* of Moses and of Aaron, who was consecrated to the LORD. The earth opened up and swallowed Dathan; it buried the company of Abiram. Fire blazed among their followers; a flame consumed the wicked'(emphasis added).[12] This psalm tells us that the specific sin of Korah and his followers was envy. Korah's own role as caretaker of the precious articles within the temple was not enough. His failure to understand the significance and importance of his particular role in the community led him down the covetous path. He envied the fact that Aaron was consecrated to the LORD as a priest and he was not. Rather than glorifying and worshipping God, Korah was concerned with his own glory. Moses rightly understood that Korah's true argument was with God. Aaron was priest only because God, the master Potter, had formed him for the role. In himself, Aaron was

12 Psalm 106:16-18

just a piece of clay in the Potter's hands. God chose the priesthood for Aaron because of His good pleasure, not because of Aaron's goodness or greatness. Korah's rebellion and anger, while turned towards Moses and Aaron, was truly directed at the way God was choosing to use Korah within the community of Israel.

Korah Took

In this passage, it is easy to observe the many ways Korah's coveting took from others. His own family was swallowed by the earth and taken to the grave alive because of his sin. His faithlessness encouraged others to rebel and led to their death by the consuming fire of the Lord. Most of all, he took glory from God by failing to rejoice that he was a part of the community of Israel. Compare Korah's actions with David's worship as he declares, 'Better is one day in your courts than a thousand elsewhere; I would rather be a doorkeeper in the house of my God than dwell in the tents of the wicked.'[13] David delighted that he was allowed by grace to come near to God. He would take any role, given that he might dwell in God's courts. Korah's willingness to disobey God's command demonstrated that his desire for greatness had nothing to do with God's glory, but was centered on self-promotion.

Korah Hid

Korah hid his own pride and envy by claiming that Moses and Aaron were actually the prideful ones. He accused them as he questioned, 'Why then do you set yourselves above the LORD's assembly?'[14] As often happens, we observe our own sin readily in others, while failing to see it in ourselves. Pride and ambition swirled anxiously in Korah's heart, so he believed it must be true of Aaron and Moses. Korah rightly

---

13 Psalm 84:10

14 Numbers 16:3

understood that the entire community was set apart to be the Lord's people. However, within God's people, He gives distinct callings, gifts and abilities to serve the body. Some within Israel were to lead, while others were called to follow. God had called Aaron to the role of the priesthood. While Aaron led in humble obedience, Korah rebelled with a prideful disregard for God's commands. His attempt to hide his own sin by wrongly accusing Moses and Aaron was met with the clarifying and absolute justice of God. God revealed the sin of Korah and his followers while showing all the people that both Moses and Aaron led by God's command.

While the church does not have the same temple regulations as the Levites, we are promised that each believer has gifts and abilities to serve God's kingdom. Just like Korah, we can often believe that our own gifts and abilities are not significant and begin to covet the abilities of those around us. As we engage in this pattern of seeing, coveting, taking and hiding, we will fail in our love for the Lord as well as our love for our neighbor. In the next section, we will observe this pattern in our own lives and then conclude the chapter by considering the truths we need to put on in order to have a right understanding of our gifts and abilities.

We See

Many of us are like the Little Rabbit who wanted red wings. We spend our days observing others and wishing to become like them. One friend is a wonderful hostess. Another friend organizes with precision. One friend has an amazing ability to serve others. Another friend always seems to be sharing the gospel with those around her. We hear one woman praise another woman and we begin to wonder, 'Am I significant to anyone? Do I make a difference?' We start to believe that if we were gifted in a particular way, we would then have the love, admiration, respect and honor we desire. We see clearly how God is using others, but we wonder if we really have any impact on those around us.

As we consider our seeing, let me begin by saying that it is good to observe the many ways God uses others to build His kingdom. As I consider my different friends, I am always amazed at how God brings so many different people together, in just the right way, to provide for His church. Our problem in seeing what God is doing with others comes when we fail to believe that He has also gifted us uniquely for a role in His church. If our seeing is mixed with unbelief, we will become people full of despair and discouragement.

Another problem that can occur as we consider abilities within the church results from wrongly placing too much value on certain roles and people. If we only esteem leadership or teaching roles, then it is clear we have an incorrect view of giftedness within the church. Paul uses the analogy of the physical body in 1 Corinthians 12 to describe the way our different abilities come together to form the church. Each of us needs a variety of parts in order for our body to work. If I was made up with twenty fingers and no toes, I might be able to type faster, but I wouldn't be able to walk very well. We are given different abilities, some more obvious than others, so that the church will be a living, loving and working body. When our eyes become focused on certain gifts and abilities, with an incorrect view of their significance, then most likely we are well on our way to coveting.

We Covet

It is a good thing to want to be used by God to build up His church. We should eagerly desire to see His kingdom advance and grow. Our problems in this area begin when our desires shift from God's glory to our own glory. Paul warned the Philippians that 'some preach Christ out of envy and rivalry.'[15] However, a heart that longs for God's glory can be content serving God in a variety of ways. I know many mothers who spend their days cleaning toilets, wiping mouths and folding

15 Philippians 1:15

laundry. In these simple acts of service to their family, they are faithfully building God's kingdom. My friends who work as teachers, bankers, engineers and doctors are also glorifying God by their faithful labor that creates a working, functioning society. Whatever we do should be done for God's glory. If our goal is His glory, then all of our lives take on great significance. However, when we start to long for our own glory, then we begin to covet the gifts and abilities that bring personal gain. Some want to gain respect or admiration while others want love or financial security. Whatever we hope to gain, self-glorification is at the heart of our coveting.

Our coveting in this area can manifest itself in two ways. First of all, we can covet the way God has gifted someone else. It is not simply that we admire their abilities, but that we have an inordinate longing to be gifted like that person. We question God, wondering why He failed to make us in such a way. Like Korah, we grow increasingly discontent with God, and we may even grow distanced from the person whose gifts we covet. Secondly, our coveting in this area can also grow from dissatisfaction at the ways God is ordering our circumstances. In certain seasons of life, we may find it difficult to use our gifts and abilities. Perhaps a woman feels particularly gifted in hospitality. However, because of financial struggles, she does not have the resources to invite others over to her home. Perhaps a woman feels called to the mission field, but her husband works as a lawyer in a small town. Perhaps a woman loves organizing events to help those in need, but now because of her four small children, she simply does not have time to volunteer in the same capacity. In this sense, we are not coveting someone else's abilities, but we are desiring for God to use the strengths He has given us in a particular way of our own choosing. We are coveting our gifts to be used for our own motivations and significance, instead of submitting them to God's timing and purposes.

When we originally moved to Scotland, I wrestled with these feelings of insignificance as I struggled to find places of service in the church. In the States, I was a public high school teacher and I volunteered with a ministry, Fellowship of Christian Athletes (FCA), that reached out to students at my school. We had a growing fellowship of students, and I believed the Lord was using me at the school to be an influence for Christ in students' lives. It was exactly what I had always felt called to do with my life.

When we moved overseas for my husband to pursue his Ph.D., my gifts and abilities were seemingly put on hold. Many days, I had nothing at all to do that I deemed significant. I tried to get involved in a variety of activities, but I still missed the ministries I left in the States. One day, when I was grumbling to myself about all that I'd given up to follow my husband, the Lord pierced my heart with a simple question. The still, calm Voice of truth asked, 'Melissa, do you love me or do you love ministry? Because, if you love me, then you will love whatever work I call you to do.'

At that moment, I realized that my ministry was not put on hold; I was simply called to a different season of service. Instead of caring for high school students, I was called to lovingly care for my husband and support him in the task of completing his Ph.D. While it seemed insignificant (and completely against the wisdom of our age, which would never support a woman giving up her aspirations to support her husband), it became a place for me to serve the Lord faithfully. He grew me and taught me more in those years by showing me that the way of the cross is not in self-fulfillment and self-gain, but self-sacrifice. I came to realize that cooking a meal, cleaning a bathroom, or spending evenings alone so that my husband could write all become significant when done for the Lord.

In his letters to the Colossians, Paul offers this encouragement: 'Whatever you do, work at it with all your heart, as working for the Lord, not for men, since you know that you will receive an inheritance from the Lord as a reward. It is the Lord Christ you are serving.'[16] If I am serving the King of the entire universe, then whatever I am doing becomes full of meaning. Our covetous tendencies rob us of the joy of faithful and humble service. Eventually, they will also cause us to take from those around us.

We Take

Once this covetous root has grown in our heart, it will spill over into our actions towards others. We will take from them in a variety of ways. First of all, we will take from others around us by failing to praise or encourage their gifts. Instead of spurring them on towards love and good deeds, we sit in silence. As they use gifts and abilities we would like to have, all we can see are our own desires. We should actively and purposefully show our appreciation towards those who work diligently among us. Paul tells the Thessalonians, 'respect those who work hard among you, who are over you in the Lord and admonish you. Hold them in the highest regard in love because of their work.'[17] Our covetous desires stifle the praise, encouragement and respect we should give those who work diligently among us. We fail to think about all the sacrifices they make for the church, and we only consider how they are getting the admiration we desire. In fact, often our own dissatisfaction wells up and overflows into arguing and discord within the church. Just as Korah's coveting led him to oppose Moses, many church-wide disputes and dissensions are rooted in personal envy and rivalries among members.

Secondly, our covetous desires cause us to take from others by failing to use our gifts and abilities to encourage

---

16 Colossians 3:23-24

17 1 Thessalonians 5:12-13

the church. Instead, we pursue areas of service that we are not particularly suited for because we have deemed that service more significant. Our failure to sacrificially give to one another through humble service eventually causes us to take from each other because we leave undone what should be done. Meals that should be made to help a family in need are not cooked. Chairs that should be set up for a ministry gathering must be set up by the pastor or some other leader, already worn thin from years of service. Nursery classrooms must close because of a lack of volunteers. Many times, the same people in the church do most of the service because they are the ones willing to humbly serve in any area. When people are unwilling to serve in the nursery, lend aid on a clean-up crew or faithfully pray because it does not suit their craving for significance, then the entire church suffers as a result. Pastors and church leaders become burned out because others fail to serve. Natural gifts and abilities are not developed as effort is put into the wrong areas. If our feet began trying to act like our hands, we would waste a ton of energy and effort. Similarly, as we covet others' areas of giftedness, we will waste time and energy that could have been spent serving the body.

Lastly, and most importantly, we take glory from God by seeking to use our own abilities to bring glory to ourselves. Our covetous desires show that we want to be recognized by others. In Galatians, Paul questions, 'Am I now trying to win the approval of men, or of God? Or am I trying to please men? If I were still trying to please men, I would not be a servant of Christ.'[18] When we seek the approval of others, we hope their praise and honor will be directed towards us. When we seek God's approval, we hope that all our diligent work and labor bring Him glory. Our covetous desires come about through self-focus, with the end being self-gain. Rather than glorify Christ's work on our behalf, we

18 Galatians 1:10

encourage others to take notice of all our special attributes and labors. In this way, we fail to glorify God as we should, and we take the honor for ourselves. In fact, it was precisely this type of coveting that led the chief priests to crucify Christ. They brought Jesus to Pilate, not because they believed He was a heretic, but because they were envious of His greatness. In his Gospel, Matthew recounts, 'For [Pilate] knew it was out of envy that [the chief priests] had handed Jesus over to him.'[19] Just as envy led Eve to the forbidden fruit, the inordinate desire of the chief priests led our Savior to the cross. These ungoverned desires take and take, never satisfied and always asking for more.

We Hide

As this pattern of seeing, coveting and taking progresses in our lives, we will eventually hide from both others and ourselves. We hide our unwillingness to serve in particular areas by claiming busyness. We hide our lack of praise for someone else's faithful service by claiming, 'I'm sure she already knows how gifted she is in that area.' We hide our scarcity of service by blaming God, instead of realizing that we have allowed our abilities to atrophy by lack of faithful use. We also can hide from our own set of abilities because we think if we are gifted at something it should come easily. Any natural ability or spiritual gift will still require time and effort to use it well. Just as the natural artist, athlete or academic must paint, exercise or study to grow their talent, we should expect that our spiritual gifts will require effort on our part as we serve others. In all of these ways, we hide from our responsibility within the church and find ourselves increasingly discontent with the other members. We must actively fight this negative pattern of coveting each other's gifts and abilities by putting on a new pattern of belief. Once again, we begin by seeking the Lord to rescue us from our wayward tendencies.

---

19 Matthew 27:18

Seek the Lord

As we fight our own ambition and pride, we should look first to the example of Jesus. Paul commands the Philippian believers, 'Do nothing out of selfish ambition or vain conceit, but in humility consider others better than yourselves. Each of you should look not only to your own interests, but also to the interests of others.'[20] He then points them to the example of Jesus, telling them:

> Your attitude should be the same as that of Christ Jesus: Who, being in very nature God, did not consider equality with God something to be grasped, but made himself nothing, taking the very nature of a servant, being made in human likeness. And being found in appearance as a man, he humbled himself and became obedient to death – even death on a cross![21]

From the moment of His conception, Jesus put off the glory that was His and chose to walk as a man. From His birth in a stable, to His ministry of service, to His death on a cross, He lived a life of love and humility, always considering others' needs before His own. As we seek to know Christ and abide in His love, His attitude will begin to overflow from our lives. Daily, we need time with Him in prayer and the Word, lest we forget that He is the source of all our service and ministry. Many days, as I scrubbed my floor or cleaned a toilet, it was the example of Christ washing the disciples' feet that changed my attitude about these mundane tasks. As I worked, I would consider that the Lord of all creation chose to bend the knee and clean dirty, smelly feet. He knew full well as He served them that each of these friends would deny Him and that one of them would betray Him. And still, He washed. His example of humility and willingness to serve should spur each of us on towards a right desire to serve others.

---

20 Philippians 2: 3-4

21 Philippians 2: 5-8

Secondly, we should remember that the Lord knows our frame more intimately than we can imagine. He knit each of us together in our mother's womb and fashioned us in just the right way for His purposes. The strengths and abilities that He gave you are to be used to glorify God and strengthen the church. A. W. Tozer encourages:

> Our gifts and talents should also be turned over to Him. They should be recognized for what they are, God's loan to us, and should never be considered in any sense our own. We have no more right to claim credit for special abilities than for blue eyes or strong muscles. 'For who maketh thee to differ from another? And what hast thou that thou didst not receive?'[22]

We are simply clay in the Potter's hand, being fashioned for our part in the great story of redemption. Paul writes, 'For it is by grace you have been saved, through faith – and this not from yourselves, it is the gift of God – not by works, so that no one can boast. For we are God's workmanship, created in Christ Jesus to do good works, which God prepared in advance for us to do.'[23] Our faith is a gift, and our good works were prepared for us in advance. How can we claim any glory as our own? While we actively use our talents and abilities, we must always remember that they are given so that we will rightly reflect the glory of Christ.

Lastly, we need to seek the Lord as we use our gifts, because our service will be in vain if we fail to abide in Christ. When speaking to His disciples on the eve of His death, Christ instructed them, 'I am the vine; you are the branches. If a man remains in me and I in him, he will bear much fruit; apart from me you can do nothing.'[24] Those who bear much fruit do so only because of the strength

---

22 Tozer, *The Pursuit of God*, p. 28.

23 Ephesians 2:8-10

24 John 15:5

of the vine. If we do not stay firmly rooted in Christ, our gifts and abilities will never develop into mature fruit. As we daily abide in Christ, our goal becomes glorifying Him through simple acts of obedience, done out of love and thanksgiving. We long for our service to be a picture of Christ's service. We long to be His hands and feet, serving others so that they will experience and know the love of Christ. Christ's love compels us to share with others, all the while rejoicing that we are part of the people of God. The particulars of *how* we serve become overshadowed by *Who* we serve. The daily desire to know Christ and walk with Him fends off our destructive desires for self-promotion and self-glorification.

Desire Rightly

If we want to learn how to desire rightly in regard to our gifts and abilities, we need an image of what it looks like to use our strengths well. Thankfully, Paul paints an excellent picture for us in his first letter to the Corinthian church. He tells them that each Christian has some manifestation of the Spirit, given for the common good. He uses the image of the body, saying, 'The body is a unit, though it is made up of many parts; and though all its parts are many, they form one body.'[25] He continues by explaining two pitfalls we can often fall into as we consider our own purpose. The first comes from failing to see the importance of our own abilities in the body as we compare them to others. He uses the following imagery:

> And if the ear should say, 'Because I am not an eye, I do not belong to the body,' it would not for that reason cease to be part of the body. If the whole body were an eye, where would the sense of hearing be? If the whole body were an ear, where would the sense of smell be? But in fact God

25 1 Corinthians 12:12

> has arranged the parts in the body, every one of them, just as he wanted them to be. If they were all one part, where would the body be? As it is, there are many parts, but one body.[26]

If we want to desire rightly, we need to stop comparing our abilities with those around us. We simply need to desire to be fully what God has created us to be, knowing that we are significant because we are a part of the body.

The second pitfall Paul warns against as he uses this image of a body is our incorrect belief that we can live independently of one another. He proclaims:

> The eye cannot say to the hand, 'I don't need you!' And the head cannot say to the feet, 'I don't need you!' On the contrary, those parts of the body that seem to be weaker are indispensable, and the parts that we think are less honorable we treat with special honor. And the parts that are unpresentable are treated with special modesty, while our presentable parts need no special treatment. But God has combined the members of the body and has given greater honor to the parts that lacked it, so that there should be no division in the body, but that its parts should have equal concern for each other. If one part suffers, every part suffers with it; if one part is honored, every part rejoices with it.[27]

Each part of the body needs every other part. We should desire that every part of our body be built up and encouraged. We should consider how to spur one another on toward love and good deeds.[28] As we are all strengthened, we all benefit.

Paul then reflects on a variety of different gifts within the church: apostles, prophets, teachers, gifts of healing, helping

---

26 1 Corinthians 12:16-20

27 1 Corinthians 12:21-26

28 Hebrews 10:24

others, gifts of administration and the gift of tongues. He concludes by saying, 'But eagerly desire the greater gifts. And now I will show you the most excellent way.'[29] What is this most excellent gift of the Spirit that we should eagerly desire? It is simply the ability to *love*. Paul realizes that all of our gifts, devoid of love, are simply wasted and without effect. We should set our desires on living a life of love such that Paul goes on to describe:

> Love is patient, love is kind. It does not envy, it does not boast, it is not proud. It is not rude, it is not self-seeking, it is not easily angered, it keeps no record of wrongs. Love does not delight in evil but rejoices with the truth. It always protects, always trusts, always hopes, always perseveres. Love never fails. But where there are prophecies, they will cease; where there are tongues, they will be stilled; where there is knowledge, it will pass away.[30]

If you posses this type of love for others, you have found the most excellent way to serve the body. Eagerly desire to grow in the ability to love – it is the greatest gift.[31]

Give Generously

Our abilities are not simply for our benefit. We are to give them generously to serve others. In view of God's great mercy, Paul urges the Roman believers to offer their bodies as living sacrifices as they use their gifts.[32] As we sacrifice our own lives to give to others, we should expect to feel worn out, tired and spent. The call of the gospel is not one of self-protection, but of self-denial. We are freed from living a life centered on self so that we can live a life following the example of Christ. As we lay down our lives, we find the

---

29 1 Corinthians 12:31

30 1 Corinthians 13:4-8

31 1 Corinthians 13:13

32 Romans 12:1

truth of Christ's words, 'Whoever wants to save his life will lose it, but whoever loses his life for me will find it.'[33]

As I view the way many live life today, we seem more concerned with enjoying and experiencing life than with serving one another in love. Often, we are unwilling to volunteer, but waste time on TV shows, Facebook and surfing the Internet. Others attempt to find life by traveling, hiking, shopping or exercise. Time that could be spent building the kingdom is instead sacrificed to chasing pleasure. Our modern conveniences have not freed us up for service; rather, they seem to have entrapped us in a greater desire for ease. Lives that are lived well for the gospel are often complicated, messy and uncomfortable. Jesus wandered this earth and faced opposition, anger and poverty. He emptied Himself in order to bring people to the Father. In view of His great mercy, we should be willing to sacrifice a life of comfort and ease to follow in the way of the cross.

As we give generously, we should also expect that our efforts and abilities multiply. In the parable of the talents, we find both encouragement and warning. Jesus tells of a man who entrusted three of his servants with a specific number of talents, each according to his ability. Two of the servants doubled their efforts, to the Master's pleasure. Each servant was rewarded with his faithfulness in small things by being put in charge of many things. However, one servant failed to grow the talent given to him; he simply buried it in a field. The master replied with a harsh rebuke, 'You wicked, lazy servant!'[34] He then took the talent from him and gave it to the other servant, saying, 'For everyone who has will be given more, and he will have abundance. Whoever does not have, even what he has will be taken from him.'[35] The

33 Matthew 16:25

34 Matthew 25:26

35 Matthew 25:14-30

gifts and abilities God gives us are not to be buried away or simply used for our convenience. They should be developed and matured through wise service. One day, each of us will give an accounting as to how we managed the abilities entrusted to us. May we be found laboring in all things with a spirit of generosity and sacrifice.

Finally, as we give generously to others, we should be encouraged to know that we will have everything we need to abound in every good work. Paul writes:

> Remember this: Whoever sows sparingly will also reap sparingly, and whoever sows generously will also reap generously. Each man should give what he has decided in his heart to give, not reluctantly or under compulsion, for God loves a cheerful giver. And God is able to make all grace abound to you, so that in all things at all times, having all that you need, you will abound in every good work. As it is written: 'He has scattered abroad his gifts to the poor; his righteousness endures forever.' Now he who supplies seed to the sower and bread for food will also supply and increase your store of seed and will enlarge the harvest of your righteousness. You will be made rich in every way so that you can be generous on every occasion, and through us your generosity will result in thanksgiving to God.[36]

As we sow generously, God is faithful to increase and enlarge us for the task He gives us to complete. Our generosity with our time, talents and service will result in a harvest of righteousness and thanksgiving to God. Our labor is worth it! Nothing sacrificed for God is lost. May you be encouraged all the more to abandon the pursuit of worldly pleasure and find abundant life by giving generously.

Confess Freely

When we find that our desires for giftedness and abilities have become for our own glory and greatness, we need

36 2 Corinthians 9:6-11

to repent. Each of us will struggle with these desires as we serve. It is tempting to desire certain gifts without considering the sacrificial cost involved. We must come to the Father, confessing our sin and repenting of our pride. James encourages, 'Who is wise and understanding among you? Let him show it by his good life, by deeds done in the humility that comes from wisdom. But if you harbor bitter envy and selfish ambition in your hearts, do not boast about it or deny the truth.'[37] By confessing freely, we will let go of the bitter envy and selfish ambition that threatens our humble service. Putting on this new pattern of seeking the Lord, considering rightly, giving generously and confessing freely will lead us to the streams of contentment that flow with the fullness of life.

Questions for Personal Reflection and Group Discussion

1. Why is coveting someone else's gifts or abilities in the church a sign of pride in our own hearts?
2. Read Exodus 28:2-4 and Numbers 16:1-35. How do you observe the pattern of 'see, covet, take and hide' in the story of Korah?
3. Why do you think Korah was envious of Aaron and Moses?
4. What consequences did Korah and his followers suffer?
5. Why do people think certain spiritual gifts in the church are more significant? How does this wrong view cause discord in the body?
6. How does coveting giftedness within the church cause us to take from those around us?

---

37 James 3:13-14

7. Read 1 Corinthians 12:14-20. What warning do we find in this passage against having too low a view of our role in the body because we compare it to someone else's?
8. Read 1 Corinthians 12:21-26. What warning do we find in this passage against having a prideful view of our role as we compare it to someone else's?
9. If we are all one body, why does it make sense to encourage others in their giftedness? How does it benefit them, as well as bless us?
10. Read 1 Corinthians 12:31–13:8. What does Paul describe as the greatest gift? How can every Christian excel in this area? In what ways can you grow in the grace of loving others as described in this passage?
11. How does our failure to use our gifts in the church harm the body? What are ways the church suffers from a lack of generous giving of time and effort?
12. Read Romans 12:1-5. From what source should our service to others flow? Why should our service be full of humility?

Concluding Thoughts

Just last week, a friend emailed me to let me know about a positive situation in her life. God had answered many prayers and fulfilled her longings in a particular area. Her good news happened to come at the point when I was struggling deeply with longings in this same area that were left unfulfilled. I would love to be able to tell you that I immediately praised God for her situation and went contentedly about my day. Truthfully, I got in my car, put my head on the wheel and cried. While I was sincerely thankful for her good providence, it brought to light the difficulty of my own situation. I did not desire her circumstances to worsen in any way; I simply desired a positive change in my own situation. I found myself once again struggling with my longings, wondering how to patiently trust the Lord when my circumstances failed to live up to my personal hopes.

Slowly, I dried my tears and began to refocus my thoughts. I had been reading earlier that week from a devotional that faithfully exhorted:

> O that Christians would learn to live with one eye on Christ crucified and the other on his coming in glory! If everlasting joys were more in your thoughts, spiritual joys would abound more in your hearts. No wonder you are comfortless when heaven is forgotten. When Christians let fall their heavenly expectations but heighten their earthly desires, they are preparing themselves for fear and trouble. Who has met with a distressed, complaining soul where either a low expectation of heavenly blessings, or too high a hope for joy on earth is not present? What keeps us under trouble is either we do not expect what God has promised, or we expect what he did not promise.[1]

My initial response to my circumstances was focused on what was lacking in my earthly situation. I had forgotten the riches of my heavenly situation. I had also failed to remember Christ's words to His disciples on the eve of His death: 'I have told you these things, so that *in me* you may have peace. In this world you will have trouble. But take heart! I have overcome the world'(emphasis added).[2] Our propensity towards forgetting His actual promises and our ability to hope in what God never promised leaves us open to the swirling tides of emotions. Our goal is not to live an emotionless life. However, we must govern our emotions in such a way that they lead us back to Christ, seeking Him in our places of longing.

My tears that morning expressed the overflow of my heart. In my lament, I joined with the psalmists of ages past as they cried out before the Lord. They sought Him and asked for relief from painful trials. Contentment is not the absence of struggling before the Lord; contentment involves struggle. In fact, just before Paul tells the Philippians that he has learned the secret of being content in any and every situation,[3] he tells them, 'But one thing I do: Forgetting

---

1 Richard Baxter in *Voices From the Past*, p. 138.

2 John 16:33

3 Philippians 4:11-12

what is behind and straining toward what is ahead, I press on toward the goal to win the prize for which God has called me heavenward in Christ Jesus.'[4] Even as Paul was fully content, he *strained onward*, pressing on to win the goal of his faith. His words denote active struggle, not passive inactivity. Contentment will not suddenly descend upon us. We must actively battle the lies of the world, the flesh and the devil in order to find peace in Christ alone. In order to have present contentment, we must keep looking back to the cross and forward to heaven. The cross reminds us that Jesus loves us enough to shed His own blood. Since He has given the most costly thing He had to give, whatever He withholds is surely part of His goodness towards us. Heaven reminds us that one day all our current longings and struggles will be satisfied. Whatever is lacking here will be fully realized there.

The morning of my friend's email brought me to a new realization. At first, I simply felt failure at my tears. However, as I contemplated and considered God's promises, I realized there will be many more tears to come. My tears were the starting point that day for me to turn again to the Lord, seeking life in Him alone. They did not necessarily speak of my own lack of contentment; they simply expressed the reality of the trouble in the world that each of us experience. By the end of the day, He had changed my wrestling into peaceful acceptance. My circumstances had not changed, but once again, Christ intervened and took hold of my heart. He brought me to contentment in Himself, reminding me that there is no other solid place for my faith to rest – all other ground is sinking sand. If you find yourself continually struggling to find life in Christ alone, don't take that as a bad sign, but a good one. You are still in the fight. We should remember that the Christian life is described

---

4 Philippians 3: 13-14

as a race,[5] a battle[6] and childbirth.[7] Each of these images depicts the reality of the struggles that accompany our walk with God. They also point to the joy that is coming. A race has a finish line, a battle has a victory and childbirth results in new life. We can endure the struggle because we know that something glorious is coming.

Throughout these months of writing and research, one particular image kept returning to my thoughts. My oldest daughter, Emma, began reading the *Harry Potter* series while we were living in Cambridge, England. I read the first one years ago, and had forgotten about the 'Mirror of Erised.' Harry, wearing an invisibility cloak, stumbles upon the mirror one evening while searching his school, Hogwarts. As he gazes upon the mirror, he is surprised to see both his parents smiling back at him. He had never known his parents, so to get to see them brought him both joy and sadness, as well as an insatiable desire to return to the mirror. He was so excited that he ran back to tell his best friend Ron, so that he also could come see his parents. However, when Ron looked into the mirror, he did not see Harry's parents. Instead, he saw himself, standing as Head Boy, holding the Quidditch cup. Dumbledore, the wise Headmaster of Hogwarts, meets Harry one evening and explains just how the mirror works:

> It shows us nothing more or less than the deepest, most desperate desire of our hearts. You, who have never known your family, see them standing around you. Ronald Weasley, who has always been overshadowed by his brothers, sees himself standing alone, the best of all of them. However, this mirror will give us neither knowledge nor truth. Men have wasted away before it, entranced by what they have seen, or been driven mad, not knowing if what it shows

5 Hebrews 12:1

6 Ephesians 6:11-13

7 Romans 8:22-24

> is really even possible. The mirror will be moved to a new home tomorrow, Harry, and I ask you not to go looking for it again. If you ever do run across it, you will now be prepared. It does not do to dwell on dreams and forget to live, remember that.[8]

Many of us have a 'Mirror of Erised' in our mind in which we imagine all that we think would be best for our life. It can be tempting to visualize our desires coming to reality and spend life dwelling on dreams and forgetting to live. The prophet Jonah cried out a similar refrain, 'Those who cling to worthless idols forfeit the grace that could be theirs.'[9] By clinging to our own images of how our life should progress, we fail to see all that God is doing in the story He is writing.

However, some images and hopes can actually be life-giving. Christ gave us such a vision in His revelation to the apostle John. In the book of Revelation, John is given an account of the last days of trials and tribulations upon the earth. However, he is also given an image of what comes after the fighting ceases. He hears a loud voice saying:

> 'Now the dwelling of God is with men, and he will live with them. They will be his people, and God himself will be with them and be their God. He will wipe every tear from their eyes. There will be no more death or mourning or crying or pain, for the old order of things has passed away.' He who was seated on the throne said, 'I am making everything new!' Then he said, 'Write this down, for these words are trustworthy and true.'[10]

John also sees the river of the water of life, flowing from the throne of God. He describes it in the following way:

---

8 J.K. Rowling, *Harry Potter and the Philosopher's Stone* (London: Bloomsbury Publishing, 1997), p. 157.

9 Jonah 2:8

10 Revelation 21:3-5

> On each side of the river stood the tree of life, bearing twelve crops of fruit, yielding its fruit every month. And the leaves of the tree are for the healing of the nations. *No longer will there be any curse*. The throne of God and of the Lamb will be in the city, and his servants will serve him. They will see his face, and his name will be on their foreheads. There will be no more night. They will not need the light of a lamp or the light of the sun, for the Lord God will give them light. And they will reign forever and ever. (emphasis added)[11]

The vision of the river of life ends with the following invitation: 'The Spirit and the bride say, "Come!" And let him who hears say, "Come!" Whoever is thirsty, let him come; and whoever wishes, let him take the free gift of the water of life.'[12]

Here we find a hope to set all our desires upon. One day, this image will be our reality. May we turn our desires towards this end and cry out with John, 'Amen. Come, Lord Jesus.'[13]

11 Revelation 22:2-5

12 Revelation 22:17

13 Revelation 22:20

Enough

Helen Roseveare

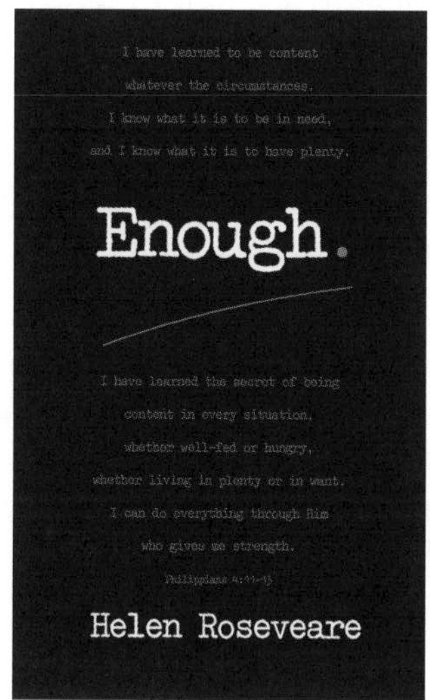

ISBN 978-1-84550-751-0

What is our motivation for serving Jesus? Is it so that we might have good health and be wealthy? Galatians 1 tells us that the wealth or health prosperity gospel is no gospel at all! However what we can find is fullness in Christ and in him we find that indeed God is enough for us! This easy to read book addresses key themes that span global cultures.

The prosperity gospel myth
Countering the view that material abundance is the sign of God's blessing and that poverty is a sign of God's curse; to distinguish between temporary, earthly benefits and eternal, spiritual ones.

Satisfaction/contentment/joy
Teaching and applying that satisfaction/contentment/joy is found in no earthly possession, achievement or position, outside of God; the fullness of Christ for every believer.

Fulfilment and purpose
Having developed the previous thoughts, this final area looks at whom we serve and not what we receive as a motivation and drive for what we do for Him.

Dr Helen Roseveare(1925-2016) went to the Congo in 1953. She dedicated her life to serving others even in the deep trials of life. She pioneered vital medical work in the rainforests of what is now the Democratic Republic of Congo, and was an internationally respected speaker with WEC ministries.

Christian Focus Publications

Our mission statement –

STAYING FAITHFUL
In dependence upon God we seek to impact the world through literature faithful to His infallible Word, the Bible. Our aim is to ensure that the Lord Jesus Christ is presented as the only hope to obtain forgiveness of sin, live a useful life and look forward to heaven with Him.

Our books are published in four imprints:

CHRISTIAN FOCUS

popular works including biographies, commentaries, basic doctrine and Christian living.

CHRISTIAN HERITAGE

books representing some of the best material from the rich heritage of the church.

MENTOR

books written at a level suitable for Bible College and seminary students, pastors, and other serious readers. The imprint includes commentaries, doctrinal studies, examination of current issues and church history.

CF4•K

children's books for quality Bible teaching and for all age groups: Sunday school curriculum, puzzle and activity books; personal and family devotional titles, biographies and inspirational stories – Because you are never too young to know Jesus!

Christian Focus Publications Ltd,
Geanies House, Fearn, Ross-shire,
IV20 1TW, Scotland, United Kingdom.
www.christianfocus.com